Jonathan Edwards, Evangelist

Jonathan Edwards, Evangelist

formerly titled "Steps to Salvation:
The Evangelistic Message
of Jonathan Edwards"

by Dr. John H. Gerstner

(Author of *Theology for Everyman*
and *The ABC's of Assurance*)

SOLI DEO GLORIA PUBLICATIONS

. . . for instruction in righteousness . . .

Soli Deo Gloria Publications
A division of Ligonier Ministries, Inc.
P.O. Box 547500, Orlando, FL 32854
(407) 333-4244/FAX 333-4233
www.ligonier.org

Jonathan Edwards, Evangelist was published under the title
The Evangelestic Message of Jonathan Edwards by Westminster
Press, Philadelphia, in 1960. This reprint is © 1996 by
Soli Deo Gloria.

ISBN 1-57358-006-6

To Jonathan Neil, age two

CONTENTS

PREFACE

Jonathan Edwards himself never wrote out in any one work his theory of the steps to salvation. There is scarcely a sermon in which he does not say something about these steps, but in no treatise or single sermon does he develop his theory. The *Faithful Narrative of Surprising Conversions*, written after the first revival of 1734, gives, as its title indicates, a narrative account of the experiences of the converted. There is, incidentally, some reflection on the underlying theory, but very little. His later treatise, written after the great revival of 1740, *Some Thoughts on Revival*, while it is far more theoretical in character than the former work, deals primarily with criticisms rather than elucidation of the principles themselves. Generally speaking, it is a defense of the underlying principles rather than a statement of them.

Likewise, writers on Edwards and on his preaching have no occasion to go deeply into his theory of salvation except, perhaps, at particular points. Miss Ola Winslow's *Jonathan Edwards 1703–1758* contains some interesting and enlightening remarks about the preaching of Edwards, but for the most part she necessarily confines herself to the more general aspects of biography. Perry Miller, in his interpretive *Jonathan Edwards*, argues the influence of the empirical philosophy of

John Locke on Edwards generally and on his preaching as well. Samuel Hopkins had reflected on the power of Edwards' preaching but confined his biography more to the man than to his pulpit work. A. C. McGiffert's biography is oriented around the revivals in Edwards' parish, so important did he consider these phases of his life, but the treatment is too brief for any thorough examination of Edwards' message. Ralph Turnbull has recently published a work, *Jonathan Edwards the Preacher,* in which he brings together many pieces of information about the training and message of Edwards and gives a very sympathetic and enlightening presentation of Edwards' evangelical labors. Nevertheless, Turnbull's work is based largely on the published sermons of Edwards, and he does not find occasion to go into the details of Edwards' theory of evangelism. It may be said of other books and innumerable articles, therefore, that they deal with matters other than those under consideration here.

In the present volume the sermon manuscripts, on which this study is largely based, are indicated expressly or by the inclusion of their text in parentheses. For example, " (John 3:8) " indicates that the sermon on that text exists in manuscript form at Yale; " (II Peter 1:19; Andover) " means that the sermon on that text exists in manuscript at Andover Newton Theological Seminary. When the reader sees a reference, such as " Matt. 7:22," not enclosed in parentheses, that means a mere citation of the text, not a sermon on it. A question mark in parentheses indicates that the preceding word is uncertainly deciphered. Such a question mark without parentheses signifies an undeciphered word. A bracket indicates a word supplied by me.

In all cases, I quote from the manuscripts if they are extant and available, unless the sermon was published in Edwards' own lifetime and therefore, presumably, had his editorial supervision (in which case I indicate this by a note). There is considerable difference between the original manuscripts and the various editions of them that have appeared since Edwards' death. In a great many instances the phraseology of Edwards is altered, and in some cases the very thought itself. When the manuscript is not extant, I resort first to the original Worcester edition of 1808 (*The Works of President Edwards*, Worcester, 1808, 8 vols.). This is designated simply as *Works*. If the sermon is not in manuscript or in the Worcester edition, I use the Dwight edition (*The Works of President Edwards: With a Memoir of His Life;* New York, 1829, 10 vols.). This is designated as Dwight *Works*.

I acknowledge deep gratitude to Yale University's Sterling Library and to the Yale University Press (which has the sole permission to publish the Jonathan Edwards manuscripts in the current edition of his *Works*) for their kind permission to use the unpublished documents herein cited. Without their permission, this study could neither have been made nor published. I wish to acknowledge, also, the kindness of Andover Newton Theological Seminary in making its collection of Edwardean manuscripts available, through the Sterling Library, to those participating in the edition of the *Works*. The Rare Book Room staff at Sterling Library has given me every courtesy and assistance.

In the nature of this research there were few who could help me. It was a pioneer work in a largely unexplored region; I was on my own. But I am especially thankful to those who made it possible for me to be on my own: my school and my family. I am grateful to Pittsburgh-Xenia Theological Seminary for giving me a sabbatical leave, most of which was spent poring over the vast corpus of manuscript sermons. I am grateful to my wife, who played father and mother to our three children so that I could give my undivided attention to this research which I regard as much hers as mine. I wish also to thank the faculty and students of Western Theological Seminary in Pittsburgh, the ministers of the Christian Reformed Institute, and the members and friends of Knox Presbyterian Church in Toronto who listened patiently and responded discriminatingly to some of the following chapters.

In conclusion may I call the reader's attention to a significant limitation in the present book. This volume is a monograph and, as such, highly restricted in character. The reader will be disappointed if he seeks to find anything in the following pages about the preaching habits of Edwards, his pulpit delivery, the structure of his sermons, the pattern of his pastoral work, his revivals, or the like. These matters are handled by other writers and elsewhere by me. This book concentrates on one point and one point only: " *The evangelistic message of Jonathan Edwards.*"

J. H. G.

CHAPTER

I

INTRODUCTION:
THE PREDESTINARIAN EVANGELIST

IT IS surprising how many men, learned and unlearned, suppose that if a preacher believes in predestination, he is not an evangelist or if he is an evangelist, he does not believe in predestination. Predestination by God is thought to preclude the possibility of decisions by men. Decisions by men are thought to be inconsistent with predestination by God.

As a matter of fact, however, predestinarian preachers have usually been evangelistic preachers. The reverse is also often the case: evangelistic preachers are very frequently predestinarians. This observation is notably true of the history of preaching in the United States.

Jonathan Edwards (1703–1758) is probably the best example in this country of a predestinarian evangelist. This New England Puritan preached, with equal vigor and insistence, the decrees of God and the responsibility of men. Indeed, he preached the necessity of human response so vigorously that some scholars maintain that he had broken with the Calvinistic tradition. Nothing could be farther from the truth. From the beginning to the end of his ministry he maintained the absolute sovereignty of God. It is the purpose of this volume to show how he combined these two doctrines.

There is a misapprehension of Edwards' preaching in the

13

opposite direction also. That is to say, there are some scholars who think that the covenant doctrine of the earlier Puritans was inconsistent with the high Calvinism of John Calvin. These " covenant theologians," it is supposed, unconsciously undermined the doctrine of unconditional election and prepared the way for Arminianism. Jonathan Edwards is seen, according to this theory, as a pure Calvinist who called the New England tradition back to Geneva and away from covenant theology. But it will be evident, especially in Chapter XIX, that Edwards was himself a covenant theologian and saw in it no compromise whatever with Arminianism.

Actually, Edwards was a " both/and " theologian — both a covenant and a Calvinistic theologian. He was neither merely a predestinarian, nor merely an evangelist. He was a predestinarian evangelist. The fixity of the divine decrees in no way altered the responsibility of men, he contended. It was, he preached, a mark of human perversity and blindness or Satanic guile to think so. He pressed his hearers for decision and warned them against prevarication because of theological quarrelings and quibbles against God. He did not say, as Calvin had said, that hell was made for the overly curious, but he inferred it often.

How Edwards conceived of the steps to salvation within the framework of divine decrees and without any violation of the decrees, we will consider throughout. It may be in order, at the very beginning, to show that Edwards was such a preacher. And this can best be shown, perhaps, by a glance at his preaching on Paul's epistle to the Romans.

Sermons on Romans were a natural occasion for Edwards to set forth the actuality of the divine decrees and the necessity of human action. A number of them are devoted to a consideration of the matter. The sermon on Rom. 9:18 may serve to illustrate his approach.

" God doth exercise his sovereignty in the affair of men's eternal salvation " is the conclusion Edwards draws from Paul's instances, cited in the preceding verses, of divine preferences even among the descendants of Abraham. After stating this " doctrine," the preacher first asks what sovereignty is. It is God's absolute, independent right of disposing of his creatures to his purpose. It is unconstrained as God acts according to his mere good pleasure. And this sovereignty is without proper obligation because God has independent right to his creatures. The implication of such a right is that God may bestow or withhold salvation without prejudice to any of his attributes. If he is bound by anything — such as keeping his promises — this is only because he has sovereignly chosen to make such promises. Edwards then shows that it may be consistent with the justice, mercy, majesty, and truth of God to save or to damn. In this discussion he has in view the sacrifice of Christ which satisfies divine justice and repairs the divine majesty. " Since Christ has wrought out the work of redemption and has fulfilled the law by obeying and suffering now there is none of mankind but what he may save without any prejudice to any of his attributes . . . " Without this grace, God's justice and other attributes require damnation.

What is God's right to do, is also his pleasure to do, Edwards continues. He not only may save some, being determined solely by his good pleasure, but he actually does so. He does so by giving the means of salvation to some nations and individuals while withholding them from others. Where God does give the means of grace, he continues to exercise his sovereignty by making them effectual or not, as he pleases. In the very same family he saves and damns. In some instances he saves where there are few means of grace and, on the other hand, permits to perish in the midst of spiritual abundance. He saves some heinous, indifferent sinners and permits some

" seekers " not to find. " Some are converted and saved that never had so great sins as some that nowithstanding perish."

There are two basic reasons for God's exercise of sovereignty in the salvation of men. The fundamental reason is God's purpose to reveal all his attributes in the creation. He can reveal no one attribute perfectly in intensity, but he does make an extensive revelation of his total being, and one ingredient of his deity is sovereignty — absolute and independent. The second reason given is only a modification of the first. The greater the creature over which the sovereignty is exercised, the clearer the revelation of this sovereignty. Hence God exercises it over the souls of men and angels as well as over the lower creation.

Since Edwards found this doctrine a peculiarly successful means of conversion, we are interested to see how he makes application of it to his hearers. First, they are to learn how utterly dependent they are on God. Second, they are to adore the awful and absolute divine sovereignty. Third, they are, therefore, to exalt God in the Father, Son, and Holy Spirit, for his sovereignty is the aspect of his grace most honored in the Scripture. And let us marvel at the condescension of the sovereign God who has chosen to bind himself in covenant. Avoid presumption, on the one hand (for God is sovereign) , or discouragement, on the other (for God is gracious) . The greatest sinner among you may be saved — if God please — is the evangelistic conclusion of the matter. And men will be saved, he infers, when they recognize that God alone can save them, but only if he pleases. The sermon ends on a note of encouragement. " Let you be whatsoever you will God can . . . greatly glorify himself in your salvation."

In this volume we are concerned to trace the steps by which the sovereignty of God is demonstrated in the salvation of men. The sermon on Rom. 8:29 is entitled "The things which God doth for the salvation and blessedness of the saints are like an inviolable chain . . ." But this "inviolable chain" begins with the eternal covenant of redemption. Its next links are the creation of the universe and the Fall of man. At the moment of the fall the actual application of this covenant to the elect begins. We shall see how it is applied in the outward call of the Word of God (the point at which we begin our narrative in the next chapter) and through the various workings of the Spirit of God, from conviction to conversion. We shall note all the intermediate steps between and the ways men take that do not issue in salvation at all, although they begin hopefully in that direction. We shall consider the way of seeking and the use of the means of grace. Further, we shall see how the Word of God comes alive in the elect in the moment of illumination, as they are re-generated and saving faith is wrought in them. That this faith is a true faith and, if so, that it is a persevering faith, we shall also notice as well as what the marks of a genuine work of grace in the soul are and how we may judge them and thereby find assurance of our saved state and, perhaps, that of others. These are Edwards' links, or steps, to salvation. And they are all set within the divine framework of the eternal covenants, which we shall study in the final expository chapter.

THE DIVINE INITIATIVE

THE FIRST STEP in man's salvation is taken by God. There is a " divine initiative " not only in regeneration, but long before that when the dead and sleeping soul is first disturbed. This outward call may or may not be followed by an inward call, but it always precedes that inward call if given. And this divine initiative, or this first divine call, which must always begin the process that may issue in salvation, is the Word of God.

There is, however, a sense in which God calls men by nature and conscience before, and independently of, the Bible. Jonathan Edwards agreed with the psalmist: " There is no speech where their voice is not heard " (Ps. 19:3). He recognized this call which God gives to all men. In one sermon he seems even to intimate that the heathen might haply feel after God and find him (Acts 17:27).

This notion that men might find God through the call of the cosmos is not developed, and everywhere else the heathen are pitied for their hopeless condition apart from the revealed means of grace. There are ten thousand wrong ways that men may discover but they can never learn the right way without the Bible to direct them (Gen. 6:22). The Greeks understood many things but not the way of salvation, because, unfortunately, they never received the Word of God (Rom. 14:7). *Man's Natural Blindness in the Things of Religion* is the title of a famous sermon on Ps. 94:8-11. " Why," Edwards asks, " has it never happened, that so much as one nation, or one city or town, or one assembly of men, have been brought to tolerable notions of divine things, unless it be by the revelation contained in the Scriptures? " He speaks of the " circumstantial unbelief " of the heathen and papists (which he contrasts with the yet greater wickedness of the more willful unbelief of people in Christian countries). In the sermon on Matt. 13:23 he says explicitly that it is not possible that the heathen could be converted. It was a sign of God's wrath against the heathen world that he abandoned it, removing himself and his ordinances while they perished (Rom. 1:24).

Although nature affords a light that leaves men inexcusable in their unbelief, faith itself comes only through the hearing of the Word of God, the Bible. The understanding of the Word is the root of fruitfulness (Matt. 13:23). Specifically, the second doctrine in this series is that " the knowledge and understanding of the Word of God is the root and foundation of fruitfulness." The Bible, Edwards explains, must be understood if men are to be saved. They are rational creatures and must grasp the message that God gives in the written Word. If this were not so, he continues, the heathen could be converted as well as others. But they are not converted because they never hear this necessary Word. It is not possible to know the excellency of God until one first knows God as he reveals himself. This will be discussed much more fully later in relation to the divine and supernatural light.

In the spirit of Rom. 10:13 f., Edwards, as well as Paul, finds that the necessity of the Word of God for salvation implies the necessity of the preacher of the Word as well. If faith comes by hearing, the question must follow: " How shall they hear without a preacher? " ch. 10:14. " The labors of faithful ministers are the principal means God is wont to make use of for the conversion of the children of the church, and so their espousals unto Christ, 2 Cor. xi. 2." (Isa. 62:4-5; *Works*, Vol. VIII, p. 337.) This is a constantly repeated teaching of Puritanism, as may be seen, for example, in the statement in the Westminster Shorter Catechism: " The Spirit of God maketh the reading, but especially the preaching, of the Word, an effectual means of convincing and converting sinners, and of building them up in holiness and comfort through faith unto salvation " (answer to question 89) . This conviction accounts for Edwards' respect for, and stress on, the necessity of an ordained ministry and opposition to exhorters and lay, not to mention female, preaching, even when many ministers were opposed to the revival and many lay preachers were advocating it vigorously.

If preaching of the Bible be so vital to salvation, it is not surprising that Edwards considered a famine of the Word of God the greatest of disasters, far worse than any other divine visitation whatever (Amos 8:11) . " By the word of God," he explains, " I mean, as is meant in the text, the outward means of grace; of which the Word is the chief and the soul of the rest." The Sabbath and the sacraments, for example, are only means of grace by virtue of the Word preached in them. God has inflicted awful judgment not only on the heathen but on many Christian communities, removing their " candlestick." Thus the Word of God has been taken from the Jews, and from Galatia, Corinth, and Philippi, and church after church has fallen under the antichrist. Not only the hearing of the Word of God, but the hearing of it soundly preached, is necessary, according to Isa. 66:10-11.

Edwards further observes that this judgment, namely, be-

ing deprived of the Word of God, is far worse than a temporal
judgment, not merely because of its eternal effects, but because it is not easily detected as is a temporal affliction. People thus abandoned do not have a sense of their misfortune
and misery as would be the case were they afflicted bodily.
Rather, they are " walking corpses," not even recognizing
their need to pray. So they walk into the greatest, eternal
danger with the least possible awareness of the tragedy.

We noted above, incidentally, that Edwards preached the
necessity of sound preaching. The inviting Word of God must
be the true Word of God. Edwards never entertains the notion that God works by means of error (Ps. 89:6). " The receiving right doctrine concerning God and Christ are necessary in order to a right temper of mind toward them." (Isa.
5:20.) Consequently there is real danger in not examining
religious knowledge, he teaches, citing Isa. 29:12 in support.
While mere orthodoxy is not enough, a minister's orthodoxy
is essential. Controversies to maintain the truth are therefore
important. While these make matters more difficult for lay-
men, essential truths are still within the capacity of all. And
" it concerns all that live under the gospel to be determined
in their own minds who that Jesus was about whom there was
so much ado among the Jews in the days of Pontius Pilate."
(Matt. 16:15.)

The Bible and its preachers unite in inviting all men to
salvation. The sword that barred Adam and Eve from re-
entering Paradise after their expulsion has been removed by
the death of Christ. The way is no longer closed but is open
to men once again. And the Bible appeals to all to take freely
of the accessible eternal life (Gen. 3:24). Especially, " sinners
under concern and distress of mind about the condition of
their souls ought to take encouragement from the infinite
mercy of God in Christ." (Acts 16:29.) Most sinners are

serene in their sins and go unperturbed to hell, but not all. Some are awakened; for these there is great comfort and encouragement in the Word of God. " No man that hears the glad tidings of the infinite mercy of God in Christ ought to be discouraged." On the basis of this gospel the Bible everywhere tells men to take encouragement. The call is " to sinners universally " (Rev. 3:20). Many are sinking into discouragement, preached Edwards in 1735–1736 (Mark 10:49), thinking that God will not have mercy. But no one should assume this although he cannot know whether he is elected before he comes. He will never be blamed for coming, and a long and tender appeal by Edwards to his congregation follows. Indeed, even if the sinner perishes he will be less miserable in hell because he sought salvation (Matt. 5:22).

The invitation of the Bible is universal and genuine; all men should respond to it. " They are blessed persons that hear the gospel of Christ and are not offended in him." (Matt. 11:6.) Many unfortunately are offended, stumbling at what they think are inconsistent or incredible or insufficient or undesirable features in the gospel. But, Edwards warned in a very early sermon, " When we have heard the word of God we ought to give earnest heed that we don't lose what we have heard " (Heb. 2:1).

Not only does the Bible itself invite sinners to salvation, but the Spirit works in the heart to convince men to accept the invitation. Like the Bible itself, Edwards represents the various members of the Godhead as inviting the soul. Thus, in a sermon on Luke 15:18 f. it is God (the Father) who invites; in Rev. 3:20 it is Christ who stands at the door of the heart and begs for admission; in Luke 15:18 f., again, it is the Holy Spirit who strives. But principally it is the Holy Spirit who is represented as the one who presses the invitation on the conscience of the hearer. When Edwards mentions the

other persons of the Godhead as doing this he does so because he is thinking of their oneness of substance with the
Spirit. Speaking personally, it is the Spirit who witnesses
along with the Word.

The Word of God and the Spirit of God closely collaborate
in the gospel invitation. The Spirit strives as the Word invites. Like a friend urging the acceptance of an offer, the
Spirit works to convince the sinner to receive the Word of
God (cf. sermons on John 16:8). While the Spirit sometimes
strives with men apart from the Bible, he never strives so
much, nor successfully, apart from it.

CHAPTER

III

JUSTIFYING A SCARE THEOLOGY

I T IS in this context of God's inviting sinners to salvation
that Edwards' preaching of hell is best understood. Edwards pictured "the kind of hell an infinite God would
arrange who was infinitely enraged against a human being
who had infinitely sinned in rejecting God's infinite love."
"It is true," says Clarence Henry Faust, "that Edwards was
much more than a sensational preacher of hell-fire sermons,
but no fully rounded picture of the man can disregard this
aspect of his work." Joseph Haroutunian in his *Piety Versus
Moralism* also acknowledges that Edwards meant what he
preached.

While others may have preached this doctrine as often or
as vividly as Edwards, none of them, in their sermons apparently ever approached the rational demonstrations of Edwards. What must have been especially terrifying to Edwards'
audience listening to his merciless pictorial representations of
the pit was the realization that they were not hearing a sensa-
tionalistic ranter striving for an effect, but a prodigious and
cool intellect driven by the purest moral earnestness seeking
to approach some adequacy of representation for a transcend-
ently awful fact.

" 'Tis in itself most rational to suppose that wicked men

should be most extremely and eternally miserable in another world " (Matt. 23:33) is typical of Edwards' rationalistic hell sermons. Edwards plunges into his argument, first showing the rightness of sinners being punished, and then of their being extremely and eternally miserable. In support of punishment in another world, he advances the point that there is no adequate or proportionate punishment in this world. Some of the most wicked have the least evidence of divine wrath; some of the least wicked have the most. He apparently agrees with Augustine's sentiment that there is just enough judgment in this world to indicate that there will be a greater one in the world to come, but not enough judgment here to make judgment in the next world unnecessary.

Supposing a righteous God must punish wicked men, how does Edwards argue that this punishment must be eternal? Sin, he says, is enmity against the Giver of all being. It is rational to suppose that this would incur the hatred of this great Being and that this Being's hatred and wrath would be as infinite as He is. The sermon on Rom. 3:19 enters somewhat thoroughly into this difficult theme.

Sereno Dwight wrote that the discourses that, beyond measure more than any others that Edwards preached, had an immediate saving effect were several from Rom. 3:19. " The sermon . . . literally *stops the mouth* of every reader, and compels him, as he stands before his Judge, to admit, if he does not feel, the justice of his sentence. I know not where to find, in any language, a discourse so well adapted to strip the impenitent sinner of every excuse, to convince him of his guilt, and to bring him low before the justice and holiness of God. According to the estimate of Mr. Edwards, it was far the most powerful and effectual of his discourses, and we scarcely know of any other sermon which has been favoured with equal success." (*Works*, Vol. I, pp. 141–142.)

This is the only sermon on Romans which was published in Edwards' lifetime. Its popular title is *The Justice of God in the Damnation of Sinners*. Edwards' actual doctrine is: " *'Tis just with God eternally to cast off, and destroy sinners.*" I do not know whether the title by which the sermon has been known since the first edition was Edwards' own or the publisher's.

The sermon begins with a review of the first part of the epistle to the Romans. Edwards reminds us that this part of Paul's letter was written to show that all men stood condemned, Gentiles and Jews alike. The words of ch. 3:19 sum it all up: " That every mouth may be stopped." From this Edwards moves to his doctrine, which he develops by two considerations: man's sinfulness and God's sovereignty.

First of all, the " infinitely evil nature of all sin " is shown. This is argued by saying that " a crime is more or less heinous, according as we are under greater or lesser obligations to the contrary " and then going on to maintain that " our obligation to love, honor, and obey any being, is in proportion to his loveliness, honorableness, and authority." From this it is quickly apparent that there is infinite obligation to obey God and that disobedience is infinitely heinous and, if infinitely heinous, deserves infinite punishment. In answer to an objection against such punishment on the ground of the certainty of sin, Edwards presents a principle that is the thesis of his great treatise on the *Freedom of the Will:* " The light of nature teaches all mankind, that when an injury is voluntary, it is faulty, without any manner of consideration at what there might be previously to determine the futurition of that evil act of the will."

Next Edwards considers the sovereignty of God in the punishment of sinners. First, God's sovereignty relieved God of any obligation to keep men from sinning, in the first creation. Second, it was also God's right to determine whether every man should be tried individually or by a representative. After the Fall, God had a sovereign right to redeem or not to redeem, and to redeem whom he pleased if he pleased. The rest of the sermon, approximately one fourth, is given over to a probing application which, it was not surprising, found many out. Much of it is a development of the opening words, " This may be matter of conviction to you, that it would be just and righteous with God eternally to reject and destroy you." Edwards ends with great encouragement to the redeemed.

Edwards himself gives the cue to his eschatological preaching. Speaking of the imprecations of the Bible, he observes: " We cannot think that those imprecations we find in the Psalms and Prophets, were out of their own hearts; for cursing is spoken of as a very dreadful sin in the Old Testament; and David, whom we hear oftener than any other praying for vengeance on his enemies, by the history of his life, was of a spirit very remote from spiteful and revengeful. . . . And some of the most terrible imprecations that we find in all the Old Testament, are in the New spoken of as prophetical, even those in the 109th Psalm; as in Acts 1:20. . . . They wish them ill, not as personal, but as public enemies to the church of God." Apparently, therefore, Edwards regarded himself as the spokesman of God in these sermons. He warned, in God's name, of what would happen to the impenitent; he does not himself wish it to happen.

As a matter of fact, and herein Edwards suffers most unfairly, all evidence tends to indicate that his fervent preaching of hell stemmed hardly more from his obedience to God than from his deep love to mankind. Believing in the reality of hell for the sinner, what would a benevolent man do but everything in his power to warn against such an awful retribution? Some of the exhortations of Edwards are the most drawn-out, pathetic appeals to the unconverted that can be found in preaching. This is not the spirit of sadism. Ironically, if Edwards, believing as he did, had been a sadist, he would never have said a word about perdition.

If it be granted that Edwards preached his imprecatory sermons because he believed God ordained his preachers to warn men about perdition, we would still expect him to probe the purpose of God in this. Nor are we disappointed — he has much to say about the strategy of preaching perdition, but, in a word, his reasoning appears to be: hell is about all of spiritual reality that can affect an unconverted man. Self-interest, his motivating principle, would concern him to avoid such a doom.

" Natural men cannot see anything of God's loveliness, his amiable and glorious grace, or any thing, which should attract their love; but they may see his terrible greatness to excite their terror. . . . A wicked man, while a wicked man, is capable of hearing the thunders, and seeing the devouring fire of Mt. Sinai; that is, he is capable to being made sensible of that terrible majesty and greatness of God, which was discovered at the giving of the law." In an early sermon on Heb. 9:12 he informed Northhampton: " The consideration of hell commonly is the first thing that rouses sleeping sinners. By this means their sins are set in order before them. And their conscience stares them in the face, and they begin to see their need of a priest and sacrifice " (cf. the sermon on Hos. 5:15). Most wicked men who have heard of hell have internal uneasiness (Prov. 29:25). On the other hand, a principal means of being lost is thinking there will be no punishment (Gen. 3:4).

Many of Edwards' sermons illustrate his use of this doctrine in evangelistic preaching. The sermon on Jude, ch. 13, is an example. " The wicked in another world shall eternally be overwhelmed with the most dismal and perfect gloominess of mind." This theme is followed by a searching application after which the preacher has his people asking, What shall we do? His answer is, Be born again. The sermon on Matt. 23:33 on the rationality of eternal punishment follows the same procedure. In the application Edwards shows the necessity of the new birth. Unlike most modern evangelists, who would either let the matter rest once they had advised men to be born again or would assure them, in Arminian fashion, that they would be born again if they would believe, Edwards tells his hearers to repair to God if, peradventure, he may give them the gift of the new birth. This evangelist does not believe that faith is a potentiality of corrupt natures. Until God gives the disposition to believe men remain unbelieving. There is, therefore, nothing that they can do to produce regeneration. But they can seek God (and Edwards always encourages them) in order that God may, if it is his sovereign pleasure, bestow this gift upon them.

On other occasions, Edwards does not proceed from the fear of hell to the topic of the new birth. Rather, he sometimes dilates on the necessity of fleeing the wrath that is to come. Of course there is only one successful end in fleeing and that is being born again. But in some sermons the preacher is intent merely on having his people flee. No doubt they understood what was involved in this fleeing and why they were advised to do it.

The famous sermon *Sinners in the Hands of an Angry God* is interesting here. In one of the editions of this sermon we have an abrupt ending without reference to the mercy of God or hope for the seeker. This is not characteristic of Edwards, who normally preached on the judgment in order to bring people to seek salvation, not to await damnation. We find that the original 1741 version of the sermon did have a more typical and hopeful conclusion.

To those who protested against Edwards' preaching in his own day — these objections did not originate in the twentieth century — he vindicated his " scare theology " in the following manner: " Some talk of it as an unreasonable thing to fright persons to heaven, but I think it is a reasonable thing to endeavour to fright persons away from hell. They stand upon its brink, and are just ready to fall into it, and are senseless of their danger. Is it not a reasonable thing to fright a person out of a house on fire? " The sermon on Hos. 5:15 develops further this rationale of hell-preaching.

Edwards never entertained the notion that anyone could be scared into heaven. Constantly he speaks as in the sermon on Job 14:5: " There is no promise in the whole Word of God that prayings and cries that arise merely from fear and an expectation of punishment shall be heard especially if they have been willfully negligent till then." He goes farther in the sermon on Luke 16:31, *Scripture Warnings Best Adapted to the Conversion of Sinners,* by pointing out that sinners are not scared into heaven but that total fear would make them all the more the children of hell. This is the reason he does not believe it would be salutary for men to have a preview of actual hell, as awakening as that might appear to be: " It would make them more like devils; and set them a blaspheming as the damned do. For while the hearts of men are filled with natural darkness, they cannot see the glory of the divine justice appearing in such extreme torments " (Dwight *Works,* Vol. VI, p. 66) .

The question has been appropriately raised: " If Edwards recognized that a preview of hell would set men blaspheming, why did he not conclude that the preaching of hell would do the same? " We do not know that this question was ever put to Edwards himself or that he ever commented on the point at issue specifically. In any case, the answer may be found in this same sermon on Luke 16:31. In it he argues that God knows best how to speak to his own creatures. And since he has chosen to declare the truth of future judgment through the Scriptures and preaching, it is a natural inference that this is the best way. God is infinitely wise, and if this is his method, there can be no doubt in Edwards' mind about its prudence. The theme of the sermon is: " The warnings of God's word are more fitted to obtaining the ends of awakening sinners, and bringing them to repentance, than the rising of one from the dead to warn them."

This remark about the inadvisability of showing a sinner the actual hell reveals, incidentally, that Edwards sought to avoid engendering a wrong kind of fear. The sermon on Jer. 5:21-22 affords a good discussion of the two varieties of fear. The doctrine is that " 'tis a sottish and unreasonable thing for men not to fear God and tremble at his presence." In the course of defining what this fear is, Edwards finds occasion to reflect that " those that have a sinful fear of God fear God as evil but a right fear fears him as great and excellent." Thus there is a right and wrong fear of God. This wrong fear of God, fearing him as an evil and dreadful being, drives men from God. " A sinful fear makes men afraid to come to God." But, on the other hand, there is a proper fear of God, as the good and holy being that he is, and this " right fear makes men afraid to go from him." If men fear God as they fear the devil, they flee from him, but if they fear him as the being he really is, they will flee to him. It is this wrong fear or " servile fear " which is cast out by love (Ps. 119:1-3) . But love does not cast out this " dread of displeasing and offending God for this holy fear don't only dread the fruits of God's displeasure but the displeasure itself which love causes him to dread."

Putting the picture together, we get this Edwardean ra-

tionale of the preaching of hell. First, God commands it and
it is essential for a steward to be found faithful to his charge.
But, second, God ordains such preaching because the sotted
sinner is not interested in the things of the Spirit. Therefore, third, he must be shown the danger of his present condition and the impending doom that hangs over him. However,
fourth, the actual sight of actual hell would be more than
frail man could stand, so only the dim pictures found in the
Biblical warnings are suitable to awakening. But, fifth, awakening to a state of fear does not take a man out of his natural
condition, and though he be desperately frightened, as the
devils are, his most importunate prayers (if motivated merely
by sinful self-interest) only further enrage God. Sixth, and
this is the crucial point, in this awakened condition, operat-
ing only from self-interest, as we shall see, the sinner may
(and the preacher encourages him earnestly) ask, "What
must I do to be saved?" The answer to that question is not,
" Be scared to death," but, " Believe on the Lord Jesus Christ
and thou shalt be saved." But, finally, true faith in Christ is
not a mere desperate or nominal acceptance of him, as a ticket
out of hell, but a genuine, affectionate trust in him for the
very loveliness and excellency of his being. This, to be sure,
is not in man's present disposition, but he may seek for a new
heart. How a person finds this new heart we must continue to
investigate.

It would be a great mistake, we note in conclusion, to suppose that Edwards preached hell and nothing but hell to
unawakened sinners. While he thought that this was the doctrine most likely to awaken them from their " sottish " corruptions, he also appealed to their love of pleasure. All men
want to avoid pain and cultivate pleasure and can be appealed to from either angle. There is no doubt that Edwards
believed that there was more likelihood of success in evan-

gelism by appealing to the fear of pain than to the love of pleasure. But he often argued very cogently for the superior joys of the converted state. One unpublished early sermon illustrates this particularly well, though this theme is handled in many discourses. The doctrine of the Prov. 24:13 sermon is that " it would be worth the while to be religious if it were only for the pleasantness of it." One reason is that religion does not deny us moderate earthly pleasures, but, on the contrary, allows legitimate ones. It requires moderation which actually heightens the pleasure rather than destroying it. Secondly, religion sweetens pleasures because it pursues them in harmony with reason and conscience. The wicked man, on the other hand, " enjoys his pleasure at war with himself." Furthermore, the righteous enjoy their pleasures assured of the blessing of God, while the ungodly have no such satisfaction, but, on the contrary, are afraid. A little religion with a clear conscience brings more joy than a great deal with trepidation of mind. Of far greater importance is the fact that religion brings spiritual joys that are vastly superior to the joys of this world with which the ungodly are alone occupied. In the application, Edwards fights the wicked " with their own weapons " — those of pleasure — appealing to them to seek God if only for such considerations.

PREACHING TO YOUNG VIPERS

I F THE BEST doctrine to present to sinners is hell, the best
time is childhood. The number of special meetings for
children that Edwards held, as well as the diligent attention
he gave to the salvation of his own family, show his persuasion
of this point. His approach to children was basically the same
as the approach to their parents. They too were in danger of
judgment and must learn to flee from the wrath that is to
come upon them as well as upon older sinners. They were
" young snakes," no different in nature from their parents.
They too were " children of the devil." Neither can they
" bear hell among the devils," and they must beware of this
dread judgment to which they are exposed. " Supposing,
children," he exhorts, " you could now go and hear the cries
of other wicked children that are gone to hell — Come therefore hearken to me — If you won't hearken but will go to
hell . . ." (the sermon on Ps. 34:11 ends abruptly here).

" Many persons," he warns the youth, " never get rid of
the guilt of the sins of their youth but it attends them to their
graves and goes with them into eternity." (Job 20:11.) Youth
is the best period in which to serve God, but in spite of this
fact it is usually spent in vanity. God will not excuse children
nor does he forget their sins and the aggravation that they

have sinned away the best time for their conversion. Young people often quench the motions of the Holy Spirit and as a result never have them again all their lives, for God may be provoked to remove the Spirit in the beginning of their days. And even if God does not act so drastically, they put themselves under great and permanent spiritual disadvantages because the habits that they early contract are difficult to change.

Edwards used the death of young Billy Sheldon as the occasion for serious warning to the youth of his parish (Job 14:2). The boy died in the midst of the great revival in February, 1740–1741. He was cut off at such a time, said Edwards to his young people in a private meeting, to make you take full advantage of your opportunity. Very few of you, he continued, were more concerned for your souls than he was for his. He was not only deprived of further opportunity to seek salvation, but did not even have the use of his reason through much of his sickness. The exposition of the text is very brief, but the application is long and pleading. Edwards used the same sermon, with an altered application, for the funeral of his own daughter at a later date.

Another consideration that was brought to bear on the thinking of the lambs of his flock was that " early piety is especially acceptable to God " (II Chron. 34:2-3). Various reasons for this doctrine are given, for Edwards always appealed to the youth also as rational creatures and urged them to test the things that he told them, to see if they were not so (Job 20:11). First, their youth was the flower of their lives, and it was especially appropriate that this prime period should be given over to the Creator. Second, they should begin their lives with God. Third, if they do give their lives to God in youth, they have more of their lives to spend with God. Men are accepted at any time, but no matter how sincere their conversion may be, if it is late they have very little time left to give to God. This is not so with young people. Fourth, conversion in youth prevents a great deal of sin and it is therefore more acceptable than at any other time of life. Fifth, those who begin early are likely to achieve more godliness and become eminent saints. On the basis of these considerations, Edwards urges the youth to seek God. He says that God is all the more likely to bestow salvation upon them if they seek for it at this, the most propitious period of their lives.

That early seekers are most likely to find is the theme of a later sermon on Ex. 16:21: " The heavenly manna is rarely found by those that neglect to gather it till late in the day." The church is the " first fruits "; later seekers have no such promises as their children. The longer seeking is delayed the less likely is salvation to be found.

Childhood is a good time for seeking salvation, not only because youth are more acceptable to God, but because they are also more susceptible to religious impressions. " Persons when in their youth are ordinarily more easily awakened than afterward. Their minds are tender and it is a more easy thing to make impression upon them." (Job 20:11.) In another sermon he says that it is easier " to terrify a child " than an adult by setting before it dreadful things (Job 1:5) . Edwards has no intention of taking any unfair advantage of children. He will not terrify them with bugbears because they are unable to know these things are not so. Rather, he believes what he says to be true and thinks that adults should believe them as well as children, that they have no better reasons than children for disbelieving them. Children are more impressionable, he thinks, because they do not oppose so many objections and are not so preoccupied with extraneous matters that they fail to feel the impact of the awful truth.

If children are more susceptible to good impressions, they are also more susceptible to Satan's impressions (Job 20:11). If it is easier to lead them into truth, it is also easier to lead them into error. This is another reason that the careful training of youth is vitally important. If, on the one hand, the best opportunity to do them good is in their youth, it is also the most susceptible time for them to suffer harm.

Edwards preached hell-fire to the young vipers of his congregation, but he also wooed them as well. He knew that they were filled with the zest of life and wanted to get the most out of it and he appealed very directly to this desire for pleasure. Do you think that sin has some advantage? he asks his children. Do you think that it will bring you pleasure, in this world at least? No, he says, it will not. Rather, it will make you sad even in this world. On the other hand, piety will not spoil your fun, but will increase your pleasure. You are, he reminds them, inexperienced with religion now but you know this much: it is better to be at peace with God. I speak to you as reasonable creatures, he continues. You do not know that what I say is true, but try it and see. If you test these things which I tell you, you will find that they are so. You will find that religion increases rather than destroys joy. This is the burden of the application of the sermon on Job 20:11, and it runs through much of Edwards' preaching to youth.

Because of the opportuneness of youth as a time for conversion, Edwards was persuaded that it was both the most likely time for persons to be converted and the proper place for a revival to begin. " After a dead time in religion 'tis very requisite that religion revive in heads of families and those that have the care of children in order to a people's being fitted for so great a privilege as to have God remarkably dwelling among them." (Luke 1:17.) In the sermon on Amos

8:11 he especially appeals to the training of children as the sure way to revival.

Perhaps the most remarkable sermon that Edwards ever preached to the youth, at least the most remarkable one extant, was based on the incident of Elisha's cursing the children who had laughed at him (II Kings 2:23-24). After a graphic recounting of the historical incident that led to the destruction of the children by bears, Edwards presented this doctrine: " God is very angry at the sins of children." He had originally added the words, " as well as others," but crossed them out. He first shows his young parishioners that they can be guilty of a great deal of sin while children. Their hearts are naturally full of it. They hate God by nature, are children of disobedience, and there is nothing good in them, according to Ps. 58:3. " The wicked are estranged from the womb: they go astray as soon as they be born, speaking lies. Their poison is like the poison of a serpent: they are like the deaf adder that stoppeth her ear . . ." Furthermore, they are often guilty of much actual sin; they: neglect God, desecrate the Sabbath, are naughty at worship, do not seek salvation as they ought, entertain wicked thoughts, hate their parents, and fall into the snares of the devil.

God is angry with them because of these sins. " He is not only angry enough to correct (?) 'em but to cast 'em into hell to all eternity. They deserve to burn in hell forever." Their being children does not excuse them, for they have more knowledge than they practice. These " young snakes " are the " children of the devil," and God hates the devil and his children. God is particularly angry because they give the first part of their lives to the devil. God is so angry " that he sends many children to hell for these things." They are so obnoxious that he will not suffer them to grow up.

So the pastor pleads with his children to get an interest in

Christ, that their sins may be forgiven. " You all of you have precious souls. Had not I known that I should not have called you together today." Consider how angry God is with you. . . . How dreadful. You cannot bear hell among devils. . . . Consider the day of judgment. You that have played together and that have gone to school together; how dreadful to be separated or to be damned together. Then you will not play together any more but cry together. Your godly parents will not be grieved for you; nor your minister. But, on the other hand, " how joyful would it be both to you and to me at the day of judgment if you might be my crown of rejoicing at the day of judgment. If you and I that have been your minister and have preached to you and warned you might stand together at that day in glory at Christ's right hand, and might say to Christ ' Here am I and the children which thou hast given me.' "

CHAPTER

V

THE SINNER'S FIRST STEP TO SALVATION: CONVICTION

WE CONSIDER now the beginning of the process by which
salvation may come to men. All that has been so far
mentioned is preparatory to this. The preaching of the Word
is the instrument by which it is to be accomplished. But until
the Spirit of God begins to apply the Word to the hearts of
men we do not have the beginning of the sinner's experiences
that may lead to actual salvation. Without that which has
preceded there would be no such experience as that we are
about to consider; but were it not for this next area of consideration these preparations would be without meaning.

Thus far, in giving or withholding the Word and Spirit of
God, God has acted sovereignly without regard to the will of
man. Whether a man was born in a land of light or experienced the Spirit's strivings was not his to decide. And there
was no possibility of a man's accepting a gospel that was never
offered to him. But once the Word was preached to him and
the Spirit did work in him, response on his part was inevitable, and the first useful one was a conviction of the truth of
the things preached. In any case, some response was necessary,
for if a man made none at all he could not escape damnation.
Many perish because they cannot be made sensible of hell
here and do not have a conviction of its reality (Ps. 10:6).

40

THE SINNER'S FIRST STEP TO SALVATION: CONVICTION

Some men, warned Edwards, are "never effectually scared and hence they never escape" (Prov. 10:24).

Most everyone, however, under the gospel gets "impressions," at least (Rom. 11:7). I have not found in Edwards a clear distinction between "impression" and "conviction," but apparently they differed, if at all, only in the lesser vividness and depth of the former. A conviction seems to be a deeper and more durable realization that certain doctrines, especially the doctrine of a divine judgment, are true (cf. unpublished sermons on Jer. 2:23; Acts 7:51).

Convictions are human reactions to the working of the divine Spirit, who "doth the finishing strokes" on Christ's salvation. "The work of the Holy Spirit as Christ's messenger is to convince men of sin, of righteousness and of judgment." (John 16:8.) It may be that the Spirit works convictions by making the person more conscious of the glory of God, because "there is nothing like seeing what God is to make men sensible [of] what they are" (Isa. 6:5).

This work of the divine Spirit is an augmenting of the workings of men's own spirits, or minds. "'Tis from these principles of natural understanding and self-love, as exercised about their own dispositions and actions, and God as their Judge, that they have *natural conscience,* and have such convictions of conscience, as have been spoken of." (*True Grace Distinguished from the Experience of Devils,* New York, 1753, p. 31.) For, though men have lost the moral image of God since the Fall and no longer have any "sense of the beauty and amiableness of virtue, or of the turpitude and odiousness of vice," they still have natural conscience. "If a man steals, or commits murder, there is something within, which tells him that he has done wrong; he knows that he has not done right. Romans ii. 14,15." Conscience also tells him that retribution must follow wrongdoing. The Spirit of God sets in to assist the work of conscience (*God Makes Men Sensible,* Dwight *Works,* Vol. VIII, p. 55).

In the *Divine and Supernatural Light* sermon we have an even clearer discussion of the relation between natural conscience and the Spirit of God in the work of convicting sinners. It is further illuminated by a comparison of this work of the Spirit with His regenerating work. " Conscience is a *principle natural* to men; and the work that it doth *naturally,* or of it self, is to give an apprehension of *right* and *wrong;* and to suggest to the mind the relation that there is between right and wrong, and a retribution. The Spirit of God, in those convictions which unregenerate men sometimes have, assists conscience to do this work in a further degree, than it would do if they were left to themselves. He helps it against those things that tend to stupefy it, and obstruct its exercise. But in the *renewing* and *sanctifying* work of the Holy Ghost, those things are wrought in the soul that are *above* nature; and of which there is nothing of the like kind in the soul *by nature;* and they are caused to exist in the soul habitually, and according to such a stated constitution or law, that lays such a foundation for exercises in a continued course, as is called a *principle* of nature. Not only are remaining *principles* assisted to do their work more freely and fully, but those *principles* are restored that were utterly destroyed by the fall; and the mind thence-forward habitually exerts those acts that the dominion of sin had made it as wholly destitute of, as a dead body is of vital acts." (*A Divine and Supernatural Light,* Boston, 1734, pp. 6–7.)

So we see that this work of convicting is basically a natural work. It is the effect of the conscience of man merely augmented by the work of the Holy Spirit. It is a work of the Spirit on the unchanged nature of fallen man; it is not a change within the man. It differs in degree but not in kind from the unaided work of conscience. While Edwards makes this the beginning of the process that may lead to salvation, it is apparent that this, in itself, is not a saving activity. Men are not able to be saved without this work, but they could have this work of the Spirit all their lives without ever being saved.

All this does not imply that men are merely acted upon and not acting. " Persons ought to endeavor to be convinced of sin " is the doctrine of the sermon on Jer. 2:23. This sermon exhorts men to think much on sins, ranging back to childhood for material: men should " ransack the secret corners " of their memories as they attempt to recall and feel particular sins. One should work to grow in such convictions (Luke 15:18-19) . Precisely because it requires time and intelligent application to grow in convictions, deathbed fears tend to be futile. They have a less tendency to conversion than those that are raised by a more calm use of reason and the influence of God's Spirit. (Job 14:15.) If convictions come too late for repentance, they are " terrible."

Convictions must be carefully preserved. " If we have any regard to our salvation it concerns us with all diligence to keep our hearts." (Prov. 4:23.) Unless we do so, we cannot expect God to keep them. Twelve rules for maintaining convictions are given (Prov. 5:11-13) : Act conscientiously in the light; avoid stupefying the conscience; heed conscience and follow it; cherish its intimations; don't accustom yourself to a great deal of doctrinal disputing; assist conscience and promote its convictions; be thorough in strivings; never hide from the truth; do not be discouraged; do not quench conscience; converse with the godly; cry to God for awakening.

The resisting of the Spirit or the quenching of these convictions is perilous. There are two main ways of doing this: namely, by giving way to lusts or by directly opposing the

Spirit in his inward workings. If a person does thus resist, he brings a yet greater damnation upon himself (Ex. 9:16). Let him lose his convictions and there is great danger that he will have no more until it is too late, for the resisting of the Spirit is a " great sin " (Jer. 2:23).

At the same time that resisting the convictions of the Spirit of God is most serious, not resisting spurious convictions is also dangerous. There are counterfeit convictions as there are counterfeits of all other religious experience. The human nature is exposed to convictions of the mind that are not of the Spirit of God. The difference is not detected by an immediate intuition. Rather, we must deduce that " if there be anything that any man experiences in his mind that does not tend to his spiritual good that is not from the Spirit of God but either from the devil or some other bad cause " (Acts 7:51).

On the other hand, true convictions are almost indispensable to salvation. God is sovereign and can bring salvation immediately, dispensing with all regular steps. In general, however, " How reasonable it is to suppose it to be requisite that a work of conviction should go before conversion and not that God should deliver from so great misery without giving any sense of it." (Rev. 6:16.)

When the Word of God is preached — especially its solemn warnings — convictions come, awakening results. Being awakened, a sinner may be offended at, resent, and reject his convictions. This is nonacceptance of the proffered salvation, or hardening. He may, however, be too impressed to dismiss his convictions so stubbornly. He may be unable to shout down his conscience and so may attempt to bribe or " flatter " it so that he may feel peace again. This is the response of a false acceptance which seems to be a real dealing with the problem of the soul and the gospel but is actually only a subtle evasion of both. Some may be unable to silence conscience either by shouting or flattering and yet not be willing to meet its demands either — this is the response of indecision. Others try to compromise, granting many of the demands of conscience and the gospel, but not all — this is the partial acceptance. True acceptance is the conversion that follows, usually at the end of a long and arduous path of seeking.

CHAPTER
VI

A FATAL BACKWARD STEP:
HARDENING

I N SPITE of the convictions that come to some persons by the
Spirit of God working in conjunction with the proclama-
tion of the Word of God, some are hardened rather than softened and converted by them. According to Edwards, everyone
is affected one way or the other by these convictions of the
Spirit. He is necessarily either hardened or softened by them;
no one is the same as he was before.

I have not found a formal definition of hardening in the
sermons of Edwards, or elsewhere, for that matter. It is fairly
clear, however, what he has in mind by this term. Nevertheless, I think it will be better understood if we notice his account of the way in which hardening comes about.

Probably the unpublished sermon on Matt. 11:21 gives the
fullest description of the process by which hardening comes
over a convicted soul. Its doctrine is that "sinners under
means of grace are ordinarily more hardened in sin than the
heathen." This is not because they have a different degree of
sin to begin with, "for all derive the same degree of corruption from the first parents of mankind." One reason that those
under light are more hardened is that the heathen cannot
react so violently because they do not have so much light
against which to rebel. It is not that they are not as much

disposed against the gospel; they simply do not have so much occasion to express this disposition. This violent reaction against conscience tends to stupefy it and make subsequent sins the easier to commit.

The second reason for the doctrine of the sermon is that " gospel sinners," or sinners who have the light of the gospel, become used to religion. It no longer makes so much impression upon them. One may become accustomed to the preaching of the gospel as one becomes used to noise: after a while one hardly hears it at all. Thirdly, many ill habits form because of this repeated resistance to the appeals of the gospel. The heathen have the same principles as gospel sinners have, but they do not have as much exercise of them and therefore are not so hardened.

Finally, the enlightened are more hardened than the unenlightened because in resisting the light of the gospel they are at the same time resisting the work of the Holy Spirit who is always associated in some measure with the Word of God. In his application, Edwards says that this doctrine explains why the preaching of the Word is a savor of death to some. (It is interesting to note in passing that some were staying away from the meetinghouse because they were afraid that the Word was becoming a " savor of death " to them; but Edwards urged them to come because this was less sinful than staying away.) And he warns his people that the more they become hardened to the gospel the less likelihood there is of their ever being converted and, if this is the case, their condemnation will ultimately be far worse than that of the heathen.

The sermon on Acts 7:51 shows two ways of resisting the conviction of the Spirit whereby hardening comes. One is by giving way to some lust or sin, whatever lust it may be. The second way is by directly opposing the inward motions of the

Holy Spirit, suppressing conscience on which the Spirit operates. Edwards presses upon his people the gravity of this latter way, for it was then a time " wherein there is much of the motions and influences of the Spirit of God amongst us." This point is developed further in the sermon on Matt. 13:7 where Edwards says that the " thorns " in the parable of the sower are the lusts that throttle these growing convictions and lead to the hardening of the soul.

From this we may be able to construct a definition of hardening. Hardening is that process of reaction to the Holy Spirit's gospel overtures by which a naturally sinful and hostile person becomes more sinful and more hostile. Some of this process goes on in men who are not subject to the light of the Christian revelation, but the term, in Edwards, seems to be applied more specifically to gospel sinners.

There is a special type of hardening called " judicial " hardening. This refers to God's judicially decreeing to give a person over to hardening, withdrawing any further overtures of the Spirit of God and thereby removing any further possibility of conversion. This is tantamount to the unpardonable sin. The sermon on Ps. 13:3 makes reference to this judgment. In the application Edwards speaks to Northampton, warning some of his parishioners of this very thing. " And here to speak plainly I must needs say concerning some persons in this congregation and especially those that are past their youth and are not yet much awakened that unless there should be amongst [us] a much more remarkable and wonderful day of mercy in this town than ever has been yet that 'tis not probable that they will ever be saved. I am not about to limit the mercy of God — but what I say is it is not likely. Otherwise there is very little likelihood that you will be saved. Some may be ready to wonder that I should speak so plain — There has been almost everything to make your case look dangerous — Some will go to hell and who will they be so likely — If we don't look upon you likely to be damned who is likely? — Some of you are so little awakened now at such a day as this . . ." He continues, citing Acts 13:41 and Rom. 11:2, warning his hearers that in times of awakening in the past, some have been judicially hardened, as they seem to be at the present.

This leads Edwards to consider an objection that had been raised or that he himself was raising. If I am judicially hardened, the questioner asks, what is the use of my doing anything at all? To this the preacher gives a twofold answer. First, no one can say who is and who is not judicially hardened. And, second, he urges them to prove the contrary by using the means of grace that are at their command. Election, he observes, is an immutable decree, but this does not prevent Peter from urging his readers to make their calling and election sure (II Peter 1:10). And so Edwards tells his parishioners that if they will use the means of grace, they may prove that they are not yet judicially hardened. And then he proceeds to give them directions for the proper use of the means of grace but concludes with this somber statement: " As to those that remain yet quite senseless I don't think it worth the while to give them any directions."

While Edwards denies the possibility of men knowing whether they themselves or others were judicially hardened or not, he did find instances in the Bible that revealed that some men were actually judicially hardened. This was true of the nation of Israel when it rejected Jesus Christ.

Simon the Sorcerer was an individual who was judicially hardened and this for one particular act. " A man may eternally undo himself in one thought of his heart." (Acts 8:20-22.) Any one act, or even a thought, may be the occasion of God's abandoning a soul forever. His sovereignty alone determines when this abandonment may occur. In Simon's case it was not his blasphemies that precipitated God's judgment, but his thought that he could buy God's Spirit. Thoughts, and especially such thoughts, seem to be especially obnoxious to God.

There are three persons who are involved in the process of an individual's becoming hardened: God, Satan, and the person himself. God provides the occasion but is not the cause. Satan is a cause but only as man co-operates with his malicious temptations; he has no independent power to cause men to sin. Man alone is the only cause, in the proper sense of the word, of his own evil actions. In a given instance all three persons may be participating but in different roles. God teaches and urges men to respond morally to the situation that he sets before him; Satan maliciously suggests that he act otherwise; and man himself wills what he wills.

Although a defender and preacher of absolute divine predestination, Edwards never regarded God as the author of evil in the sense of being the instigator of it. In the treatise on the *Freedom of the Will* he discusses this question and says plainly (Part IV, Sec. IX) that God is the " orderer " of sin but not the " actor " or author of sin. " Sin," he continues, " may be an evil thing, and yet that there should be such a disposal and permission, as that it should come to pass, may be a good thing." (*Freedom of the Will,* by Jonathan Edwards, edited by Paul Ramsey, New Haven, 1957, p. 406.)

In his sermons also, Edwards is concerned to absolve God of any moral responsibility in the commission of sin. In the exposition of Heb. 2:3 (Andover copy) he puts the blame squarely on men. In the application, he faces the objection that God is the cause of sin because he does not prevent it but rather permits and ordains it. He shows the absurdity of this charge. Because God is the source of all that is good, and evil occurs only by his permission, it does not follow that he is the cause of this evil. If he were, it would mean that because God is the " fountain of all light," he must be the " fountain of all darkness." He is the author of all good and therefore he must be the author of all evil too. No, Edwards argues, it is more logical to state the matter the other way around: if all good, specifically faith, is from God, then all evil, specifically unbelief, is from another source. Man does not have the disposition to believe, but that fact does not imply that he is not the cause of his own belief. It is no argument that man cannot poison himself because he cannot cure himself. It is no argument that God can poison because he can cure, is the inference. In his *Freedom of the Will*, Edwards argues in the same vein with a different analogy. Because the sun is the source, or cause, of light, it does not follow that it is the cause of darkness because darkness follows in its absence. Surely God cannot be considered the cause of evil inasmuch as he is good and nothing but good, and nothing but good proceeds from him.

Satan is not the immediate cause of evil in human actions, although he is always an aider and abettor of it. Discussing the parable of the sower and the hard wayside soil, Edwards says that the people represented by this soil are through regarding the Word as soon as they have finished hearing it (Matt. 13:3-4). As soon as they leave the meetinghouse, the Word leaves them. Christ and the devil both go over this ground frequently. By resisting Christ, these people become hardened and thus provide an easy path for the devils. The seed will not sink into hardened ground and, of course, will not bear fruit. It bears no fruit at all; there is not even a temporary reformation. These people simply continue in sin and malice. So the devils devour this seed. This lower world is full of devils and they are ever ready for this job. They devour anything that is exposed to them. The devils snatch away the Word and blind the eyes of these people so that they never understand. Their hearts thereby become incapable of receiving any impressions. They then see nothing in preaching but entertainment on which they may pass their criticisms, if they do not fall asleep.

Jonathan Edwards always places the blame for a man's sins at the door of the man who does them. While the actions of men are eternally determined by the decrees of God, and Edwards teaches this unflinchingly, they are determined in such a way that nothing impinges on the freedom of man properly understood. The great treatise on *Freedom of the Will* was written to demonstrate this doctrine against the contingency doctrine of the Arminians. He attempts therein to show that freedom, as Arminians understand it, is a meaningless notion which needs only to be stated to make its absurdity apparent. Once having demolished the contingency doctrine, Edwards attempts to show in the conclusion of this work that although man is not free, in the sense that Arminians have supposed, he is a moral agent and his actions are truly responsible ones worthy of praise or blame.

While lacking the very close, and often very abstract, reasoning of the treatise on the *Freedom of the Will,* Edwards' popular sermons taught the same doctrine. He preached his theology and with basically the same arguments, though fewer in number and less technical in expression. For example, Edwards' celebrated sermon on Rom. 3:19, *God Justified in the Damnation of Sinners,* which has been summarized above, gives a rather thorough analysis of the origin of human sin and man's responsibility.

The seriousness of hardening is seen not only in its own heinous nature as a form of resistance against the gracious overtures of God and in its dreadful results, but comparatively, in relation to other sins of men. Thus, it is worse than Adam's breaking of the covenant of works which has plunged the race into ruin. Furthermore, it is worse than the sins of unenlightened heathen who do nothing all their days but sin and never have any hope of being converted and saved.

Choosing evil after great light sears the conscience all the more, and this is a great prejudice against making a contrary choice. In another sermon (Jer. 6:29) Edwards reminds his people that they are prone to wonder at the wickedness of the heathen of the West Indies, but warns them that if they, his parishioners, continue sinning against their Christian light, the islanders will not have half so much to answer for as the sinners in Northampton.

Why sinners react so violently to light and thereby harden themselves is not often explained by Edwards. Nevertheless, we have a lucid discussion of this matter in the sermon on Acts 13:41. Its doctrine is: " The aggravated misery of many unbelievers appears in that though they hear and see much of God's wonderful works of salvation yet they never believe but despise and wonder and perish." The experience of the unregenerate, when confronted by the phenomena of a revival taking place around them, is here elucidated. They " behold " what is going on. That means simply that they see the miracles of grace and the effects that these have on the lives of the converted. They are aware that things are happening and they are even impressed by them. Nevertheless, these things look dark and strange to them. They do not understand them at all. " He came unto his own and his own knew him not," John 1:12. So the Jews at Antioch did not know what to make of the revival that had attended the preaching of Paul. They were at a total loss.

Of course, believers do not actually comprehend the phenomena of revival either. Its full meaning eludes them as well as others. But, unlike the others, they do apprehend what they cannot comprehend. They have a partial and a spiritual understanding of the great things of God, while the unbelievers see the same things but do not see them with spiritual eyes. Thus sovereign grace is never understood by the ungodly; nor is original sin, divine sovereignty, the meanness of the Christ, the eating of his flesh, or the other truths of revelation. These are light to the " Israelites " but they are darkness to the " Egyptians." Edwards compares these blind beholders to the ancient lord who, according to the prophecy, saw the food that he was unable to eat, II Kings 7:2. So it comes about that unbelievers behold outwardly without ever understanding. Therefore, they despise and wonder and perish.

The results of hardening are numerous and awful. We have already noted that it leads to irreparable judicial hardening. But whether it eventuates in that dread judgment or not, hardening always exposes men to a danger of imminent ruin. It carries with it, also, a premonition of their ultimate undoing. And those who are guilty of it are due for an aggravated degree of divine condemnation.

" When men are so regardless of divine chastisements and corrections as to continue unawakened and unreclaimed by them it brings 'em into great danger of utter destruction." (Isa. 9:13-14.) It brings an aggravated misery in hell. This effects no ordinary perishing, terrible as that is. According to the sermon on Acts 13:41, those who perish in a hardened condition shall go to the lowest and hottest places in hell. Such persons will wish that they had never lived in a land of light, will wish that Christ had never come.

Commenting on Jer. 6:29-30, Edwards warns " that it argues great danger of being finally left of God when sinners have lived long unconverted under eminent means of conversion." He leaves no doubt that he is speaking to his own neighbors and makes special reference to their response to the preaching of their former revered minister, Solomon Stoddard. " In what a clear and awakening manner have you hundreds of times had your danger and misery in a natural condition set before you." Those who could have " stood it out " against such preaching must be " undoubtedly of exceeding hard hearts." But now the bellows of that great voice are burnt out. His work is finished. But why was he sent? Usually God sends eminent ministers to gather his elect as he sent Christ to Samaria, and Paul to Corinth (forbidding him to enter Bithynia, incidentally). So, " God sent Mr. Stoddard to this place because he had an elect people here and he continued him 'till he had done the work he designed him for." So God may be withdrawing from this generation as he did from Israel in the wilderness. And as he forsook that generation and began to work wonderfully among their children, so he may do in Northampton now. As he took his Spirit from Israel when Christ died, so he may take him from this generation after the death of Stoddard. Hardening is indeed a premonition of a possibly impending doom.

Thus, hardening is something more than the usual sinning with its awful retribution — it is an aggravated offense with an even greater measure of divine retribution. " Some persons under means of grace are in such a state that they are not only dead but they are as it were twice dead and plucked up by the roots."

CHAPTER
VII

OTHER WRONG STEPS

WE HAVE SEEN thus far that the first act of God in the salvation of a man is the outward call of the gospel. But many men repress or obliterate the conviction that results from the call of God. Hardening follows from their failure to cultivate the gracious convictions that God gives, and the results, as we have seen, are that their last condition is worse than the first. This hardening is the worst reaction that the sinner can give to the call of God. It is not, however, the only futile response. There are other wrong steps. First, some persons hypocritically pretend to believe, but actually resist. Second, still others are so affected by their convictions that they seem willing to respond, at least somewhat, but they remain neutral persons who cannot decide whether to accept or reject the invitations of the gospel. Third, others actually comply with the demands of God to a considerable extent, but not quite thoroughly or completely. Far from being immediately hardened, they go farther than a mere neutrality; but they never become real seekers. It is these three groups of persons, who take wrong steps other than hardening, which we will now consider.

This first group are those in whom hardening occurs, but not obviously. That is, some appear to accept the gospel, although, in fact, they do not. They actually are hardening themselves when they appear to be softening toward the gospel. They seem to be not hostile, but friendly to the gospel. But not all who make an outward appearance of love and submission, not all who eat and drink at the ordinances, not all who say " Lord, Lord," and not all who entertain hopes of salvation truly believe (Matt. 7:21). " Hell is full of GOOD INTENDERS, who never proved to be TRUE PERFORM-ERS: Acts xxii. 25 . . ." Such persons think themselves and are thought by others to be true Christians and may even have considerable security. In the sermon on Matt. 6:2, Edwards finds that men commonly uphold themselves and make themselves easy till hell-fire makes them uneasy. Hypocrites may have " a sort of peace in their consciences " (their consciences being not satisfied but merely blinded). They may feel comfort and joy in thinking how dear they are to a God who hates them. Indeed, they may even be expecting high degrees of reward in heaven. All this is to no lasting avail, for as the doctrine of this sermon has it: " Hypocrites will never get anything by their religion but only what they get in this world." This false acceptance brings only a false assurance. " Wicked men generally flatter themselves with hopes of escaping punishment, till it actually comes upon them." (*Works,* Vol. VIII, p. 116.)

This false assurance is usually fatal. Seldom do persons who make an empty profession and then enjoy the specious sense of security that follows from it ever become truly converted. " Conversion is a rare thing; but that men are brought off from a false hope, of conversion, after they have once settled and established it, and continued sometime in it is much more rare. " (Job 27:10.)

Men necessarily are brought to a point of decision by being awakened. Previously they had walked senselessly on the

broad road to destruction. Suddenly they are made aware of
their direction and at the same time the possibility of changing it. They may get off the broad road and enter, agonizingly,
on the narrow one. All the rational arguments clamor for the
change, but the dictates of the flesh are very powerful. In
spite of all this awakening, our second group vacillate between two opinions.

Edwards warns these awakened ones: " There are no neu-
ters in religion " (Matt. 12:30) . There can be no traveling on
both roads at the same time. Vacillation is not half religion,
but irreligion. Making no decision is the wrong decision.
Choose this day, or the choice is made for you. You cannot
serve God and mammon, Jehovah and Baal. Of what use is
being awakened if you do not rise and shine? There is no
purpose to do so much unless you do more. It is unreasonable
to be undetermined. Those who halt between two opinions
are evil men, for the duty is not to hesitate but to believe —
with all, not part, of your heart. Some of you, he laments, have
been exhorted for years but have not yet decided. In his revival sermon *Pressing Into the Kingdom* he complains of
those who were " entangling themselves about the doctrine
of original sin, and other mysterious doctrines of religion,
that are above their comprehension. If they are violent, they
are only working violently to entangle themselves, and lay
blocks in their own way. Their pressure is not forwards."
(*Discourses on Various Important Subjects,* Boston, 1738, pp.
137–138.)

" The unresolvedness of many persons in religion is very
unreasonable," declares Edwards in a published sermon on
I Kings 18:21. This Bible passage deals with the contest between the prophet Elijah and the prophets of Baal before the
people of Israel. The prophet of Jehovah was challenging his
people to make their choice between their God and the

heathen deity. Their indecision brought forth the prophet's rebuke, justly, says Edwards. For one thing, they were undecided about truth, and truth has a right to be believed, not doubted. They were also unresolved about their " portion." They could not decide between heaven and hell. Rather they wanted to have heaven but without self-denial; or, on the other hand, they wanted to have the world without hell. " They would feign divide heaven from holiness . . . sin from hell." (*Works,* Vol. IV, p. 316.)

Such indecision was unreasonable for many reasons. First, religion is most important and may not be put off. Second, people are able, if they will make up their mind to it, to determine what is best; even children can do this. Third, they have an opportunity to choose. Fourth, the choice is only between two, not many alternatives. Fifth, there are all needed helps to aid in deciding. Sixth, there is no need for delay, for there is no more information coming nor necessary. Seventh, if the person does not decide, the matter will be decided for him by God. Eighth, no one knows when the opportunity will be gone. The sermon is concluded with a solemn exhortation in which the undecided in Northampton are reminded that " God hates those persons who continue from year to year " unresolved in religion.

The third group are those awakened persons who seem to be more than neutral but who are, nevertheless, not converted. They seem to have decided to flee wrath, to abandon the old road, to break with sin. And indeed they do break with sins, with many sins, with almost all of their sins, but not all. It is as if they had begun to flee the city of destruction and have hesitated at the very gates.

There are some sinners that feign would have salvation and do many things for it, and yet there are some particular sins that they will not part with. " There are many things that they do for their salvation, though they are not thorough in doing yet neither are they wholly negligent." (Rom. 11:7.) In this sermon Edwards says that some awakened persons do moral duties, avoid vicious practices, attend on religious opportunities, receive the ordinances, and even go to the small, private meetings. Herod not only was afraid as he listened to the preaching of John the Baptist but he even had some " affections " — he heard that awakening preacher with " joy." He was distinctly on the Lord's side. Apparently only Herodias, his brother's wife whom he had illegitimately taken for his own wife, stood between him and heaven. But that was all that was necessary. He went to hell with her in his arms. His convictions were too little and too late. For a piece of fluff he would spit in God's face. This was his great wealth which kept him from entering the Kingdom of God, as the rich young ruler's had kept him. Edwards speculates that if Christ had demanded half of the latter's fortune, rather than all of it, he might have become a Christian. By inference, if the Baptist had required anything but Herodias, Herod might have been converted.

There are many, like Herod and the young man, who part with many things but not with all. Some, like Pharaoh, finally part with everything, only to regret it a moment later, Ex. 10:9. Like Agrippa, they are almost persuaded. But it would be just as well to do nothing as not to do everything. " There are some persons that wish that they had salvation and yet won't comply with the necessary means of it." (Matt. 19:22; Andover.) " They aren't thoroughly awakened, but they wish they were." (Rom. 11:7.) Being " awakened " they are weary " in " their sins but not weary " of " them. So " they spend away their time in wishing . . . and not doing and still continuing in the way that leads to destruction." (Rom. 11:7.)

Why do men do so much and yet stop short of enough? In one sermon four reasons are listed. For one thing, these convicted but not converted persons do not hate sin as sin. They hate not the nature of sin, but its consequences. As a matter of fact they love sin as such, but would have it divorced from the things that issue from it. In another unpublished sermon it is shown that they love the consequences of virtue but not the nature of it. Indeed, they hate virtue as such, while desiring the comfortable things that follow it. The sinner likes the nature of sin and the consequences of virtue. He is always seeking to reverse the divine order of things and do evil hoping that good may come. He would sow what he does not wish to reap, and reap what he has not sown. Since Herod does not hate sin as sin, he does not detest the sinfulness of having Herodias. He may have given up other sinful practices that he enjoyed, but he did not do so because he hated them. Rather, he dreaded their consequences, for he was an awakened and not a sottish person. But even though awakened and uneasy about the dangers of having Herodias, his fear of the possible consequences of that was not as great as his carnal love for her. Since he never hated sin but only its consequences, and since in this case the future consequences are not real enough to counterbalance the present illicit pleasures, Herod fails.

Second, the almost, but not entirely, persuaded do not count the cost. They suppose that by denying this and denying that their negations can add up to the Kingdom of God. They realize neither the infinity of their guilt nor the worthlessness of their denials. Nor do they realize that God requires a denial of themselves in distinction from their possessions. Little do they suspect that when they deny this or that thing for fear of the consequences they are not denying themselves at all. Indeed they are worshiping themselves in such denials.

It is their own self-interest, and not the will of God, that they serve. They do it not to serve God, but to save their own skin.

Third, they never choose God for their whole portion. They would feign have God as an appendage to their lusts. They like the prospect of a Jesus who would save them in, rather than from, their sin. God is not their chief end, merely a means to an end.

Fourth, they cannot trust that God will reward their self-denials. Edwards often addresses himself to the young people on this point. They are afraid to miss all the good things that go with youth. They are often thinking that religion is more suitable for later life when they have more time and less zest. If they become absorbed in Christianity, now, they fear, they will miss out on life. So they and all men, for this practice which starts in youth persists throughout life, are always afraid to lose their lives lest they do not find them again. And they never quite believe Christ when he says that if they save their lives they will lose them.

CHAPTER VIII

AN EVANGELISTIC APPEAL
TO AN UNWORTHY MOTIVE

W E HAVE SEEN how men react when they have received
convictions from the Holy Spirit. Some have been hardened; some have vacillated; some have only partially com-
plied. The great problem is how to appeal to sinners to seek
with all their heart a gospel that they hate with all their heart.
How is the evangelist to persuade his hearers to seek what
they are inclined to flee? To what good motive can the
preacher appeal in men who are not inclined to good motives? Or, if they have no good motives, to what can the evangelist appeal? There seems to be nothing left but an evil motive — an evil motive for seeking a good thing! It is at this
point that Edwards makes an evangelistic appeal to an unworthy motive.

What is the motive that can lead a natural man to use what
ability he does have? It is self-interest. This can make natural
men seek the good of their souls (Rom. 3:11-12) . They may
by it be led to seek for eternal, as well as for temporal, happiness. Even though this motivation is not good, some of the
ways by which men seek may be said to be right. These ways
may possess a " natural rather than a moral goodness." The
way is right or good only in the sense that it is likely to issue
in the happiness of those who seek.

The principle of self-interest is the sinners' only point of contact with the gospel which they hate. If it were not for this, there would be no relevance of the Word of God to them (Num. 13:27-28). In a sermon on Gen. 3:4 Edwards said that a principal means of bringing the lost is their thinking that by coming they will not be punished. " Self-love duly regulated," he preached in a late sermon, " is a thing of great use in religion " (Prov. 19:8). A sermon on Zech. 7:5-6 is devoted to a discussion of the relation between men's aim to please God and their desire to serve their own good.

The question may be raised, Why does self-interest not lead all persons to become Christians? Or, Why is the grace of God necessary when there is such a lever as this? This question is answered in the sermon on Num. 13:27-28. Men like some things and not others in the gospel. Many virtues tend to bring worldly advantage. This they like. However, men utterly dislike these virtues as they are actually offered. " In their esteem there is good and bad mixed, but the bad vastly outweighs. So that upon the whole they entirely disapprove. . . . There is nothing belonging to Christianity that these professors like as it is. . . . So those things in religion that natural men dislike and account evil are giants in their eyes that eat up all the good." This then is the reason that self-interest alone will not make Christians of natural men — there are too many things that do not interest them.

If men actually do become professing Christians from principles of fear and self-interest alone, they are not true Christians. A man may start the search for conversion motivated by fear and self-interest, but he can never end it that way. Self-interest may lead him to seek for a conversion, which conversion would supplant the principle of self-interest by God-interest. In the sermon on Prov. 10:24, Edwards discusses the futility of selfish religion. The doctrine of the sermon is the

text itself: " The fear of the wicked shall come upon him."
This fear of the wicked arises from conscience and self-interest. And this fear will really come upon them, for they, in
spite of their fear, are never actually awakened — are not
" effectually scared." That is, they are not scared enough to
seek God for a new heart. Since there is no virtue in their
fear, as such, nothing comes of it. Self-interest alone works
no good.

In the Rev. 3:20 sermon Edwards discusses the role of self-
interest in the true Christian life. Far from seeking our own
interest, he declares, we must, if we would be Christians,
deny ourselves. The end of self-interest marks the beginning
of Christian faith. Still, " The godly do seek their own happiness in all they do in the sense that 'tis their happiness to
do that which shall be well pleasing and acceptable to God."
The glory of God is the happiness of all those who love him.
Nevertheless, it is the glory of God at which the Christian
aims, not at his own happiness. But his happiness comes as a
by-product when he is not seeking self-interest any longer.
So long as he is seeking his own ends he never finds them;
when he ceases to seek them he has found them. It is in the
light of the above that we must think of Edwards' many appeals to seek higher degrees of reward in heaven — we may
call it an appeal to a Christian self-interest.

More particularly devoted to a discussion of the relation
between the aiming to please God and the Christian's own
good is the undated sermon on Zech. 7:5-6. The doctrine is
that " no religion is acceptable to God but that which is done
from a true respect to him." That is not a true respect to God
which springs from self-love. That only is true which has its
foundation in a high esteem for God and a sense of his excel-
lence. True worship consists in the following elements: first,
an aim to glorify God; second, an aim to please him; third,

an aim to be like him; fourth, an aim to enjoy him; fifth, an aim to have eternal life because of his promises. In aiming at these things the Christian will find his self-interest wonderfully advanced, but that must not be his aim, Edwards explains. The reasons that this should not be his aim are given in the latter part of the exposition. Among these reasons, two may be mentioned: first, there is no goodness in anything that is not done for the glory of God, for God alone is good; second, aiming to worship God in the interests of self-love implies a lie and, therefore, could not be good.

Nevertheless, though man is able to exercise his ability of himself, for his own interest, there is no merit in all of it before God. Man cannot be saved without seeking, and his seeking is the usual way in which salvation is found, but still there is no merit at all in any of his seeking. After all, this seeking is totally devoid of any formal good, as we have noted. However good these works may be in themselves, they have no goodness as related to the doer. We may call them bad good works. Hence God has no obligation to acknowledge them, much less reward them, with anything as great as eternal life. As a matter of fact, if we speak of the merit of these bad good works, they merit eternal damnation, being utterly odious in God's eyes when considered in relation to the doers. " If ye then, being evil, know how to give good gifts . . . ," Matt. 7:11. It makes no difference how long a person seeks or how many of these " good gifts " he gives or " good works " he does. If seeking is bad, a long time in it deserves no more than a little (Rom. 3:11). A thousand dead bodies are no better than one. Indeed, God has more reason to be angry with the many than with the few, considering their nature. " It is a gross mistake of some natural men, that think when they read and pray they don't add to their sins . . ." (I Thess. 2:16.) " All the while " sinners who are doing these so-called good works " imagine that they do deserve that God should pity them and hear them and help them they are meriting his hatred and fury and that God should be more incensed against them." (Luke 17:9.) " Our prayers are loathsome till they are presented by him " (Christ) " in his intercession." (Heb. 9:12.)

It may be profitable to go into more detail concerning Edwards' view of these works. Doing these bad " good works " is evil, but it is less evil than not doing them. If the sinner does not do these " good works " from his evil heart, he will do bad things from his evil heart. So he will be more evil. Bad works are certainly more bad than bad " good works."

There is an observation that needs to be made here: If the unregenerate do these bad good works pretending that they are good good works, that is certainly worse than bad good works frankly acknowledged to be such. Hypocrisy would be present in one instance and not in the other, and this would certainly augment the evil. This is the same as to say that hypocritical bad " good works " are far worse than unhypocritical bad " good works." The casuistical question remains — Which is worse: hypocritical bad " good works " or bad bad works? That is, specifically, is it more sinful for a man to keep the Sabbath, outwardly, pretending that he loves God in so doing? Or, is it better to break the Sabbath, making no pretenses to loving God? It seems impossible to construct an ethical calculus by which to evaluate two bad motives plus one good deed over against one bad motive and one bad deed. Suffice it to notice here that all these possibilities exist in the morass of moral possibilities. Edwards was not only aware of them but he preached about them. One thing on which he repeatedly insisted is that it is far less sinful, and far more likely to bring salvation, for men to do bad good works than to do bad bad works.

This leads Edwards to deal more specifically with a question that some were raising. If all that I do is wrong, why do anything? In answer he presents two reasons. First, he informs his parishioners that it is foolish to ask the question because they cannot possibly avoid doing. They would have to cease to be in order to cease to do. Second, they can do what is negatively right and avoid what is more wrong. That which is negatively or materially right, though formally wrong, is better, or less evil, than that which is both materially and formally wrong. Furthermore, he observes, it is likely to issue in saving good by the sovereign grace of God.

In other sermons, Edwards lists other advantages of these bad good works. Thus, doing them avoids the guilt of not doing them (II Chron. 32:25). At great length Edwards argues that the amount of suffering in hell avoided by doing these works is infinitely worth-while. Every sin adds an infinity of guilt and punishment, and therefore the avoiding of such is highly advisable even if the denial should never lead to salvation. " And though you never should go to heaven yet if you will live a moral life you will surely have a less punishment. . . . 'Tis not absolutely certain that they shall go to heaven but this is certain that they shall escape an exceeding intolerable addition to their eternal misery and indeed every degree of that misery is intolerable." (Matt. 5:22.) God commands men to strive to enter the Kingdom of God. If they do not, they will someday wish that they had sought it, even if they had not attained. A fourth reason is the temporal rewards that come from the doing of duties, even externally and unsavingly. Being honest although the motive is not good, our Yankee Puritan observes, brings temporal prosperity.

Only God has the ability to convert or give the desire for conversion. Sometimes natural men think they desire conversion. They say that they would be glad to be made willing. They think they are willing to be made willing (Luke 15:28-31). Edwards argues that such a statement is not sincere but indicates merely a fear of hell. If men desired to be made willing, this would show that they were willing, which by supposition they are not. For if they were willing to be made willing they would not need to be made willing. If they truly desired to desire God, that would show that they did desire God and need not be made to desire him.

Men are not willing in any sense. They are able but not willing (Eccl. 4:5; Andover). "The reason why they don't use the means is not because they could not if they were disposed but because they are not disposed." Men are destitute of faith naturally. They can reject Christ but they cannot accept him (Heb. 2:3). Men must labor to get their hearts disposed (Luke 16:16). The strong desire for the Kingdom is out of our reach, and for that reason we should be stirred up to use the means of grace that the desire may become ours. Some things are simply beyond us (Eccl. 9:13). They strive in vain who strive to make themselves new (Ps. 36:12). Their striving is not so much an earnest seeking to God, as a striving to do themselves that which is the work of God. We should strive to have God do this for us. We should seek a new birth from him (Jude, ch. 13). Men must be made willing (Gen. 24:28). And being made willing, they then make their "free choice." To use Augustine's expression: men are "free" by nature, but they are not "freed" to do good until God makes them so.

Notice how Edwards scores the notion that men are "freed" by nature: "Having heard that if ever they believe, they must put their trust in Christ, and in him alone, for salvation, they think they will trust in Christ and cast their souls upon him. And this they endeavour to do in their own strength. This is very common with persons upon a sick bed, when they are afraid that they shall die and go to hell, and are told that they must put their trust in Christ alone for salvation. They attempt to do it in their own strength " (Hos. 5:15). Having warned his people against such a notion, Edwards continued urging them " to seek to be made sensible of your misery and unworthiness," to strive against sin and labor in duty, with the prayer and hope that God will bestow saving faith.

CHAPTER

IX

SEEKING SALVATION

WE COME now to what is the most hopeful step that an unconverted man ever takes and what is the keystone of the evangelistic theory of Jonathan Edwards. When men have been convicted by the Spirit of God, and are not hardened, nor neutral, nor holding back at one point or another, they are true seekers. They are those who are determined to find the God who has stirred them up to seek him. There is nothing more that an unconverted man can do than seek, and Edwards never wearies of pleading with him to do that. The matter now passes into the hands of God alone. If men will seek, they do all that in their fallen condition they can do, and the preacher to fallen men has moved them to all that is in his and their power to do. Now the issues are with God alone. The preacher and the seeker alike await the sovereign will of heaven.

Suppose, then, that a person responds properly to the divine call; he will not refuse, remain indifferent, nor comply partly, but will, to the utmost of his ability, seek. The question is, What is the ability of a sinner who is the bond servant of sin? In a Calvinistic system of theology which stresses the inability of fallen man, what is he to do? Jonathan Edwards not only finds a certain ability in even fallen man, but he appeals to it so frequently and earnestly and evangelistically that many interpreters have actually supposed that in his preaching this arch opponent of Arminianism succumbed to that very doctrine which he did more to resist than any other American Calvinist. Actually, as we shall see, the " ability " that Edwards attributed to the sinner was consistent with Calvinism.

Before we come, in the next chapter, to the crucial question of ability, let us first note Edwards' emphasis on the necessity of seeking salvation. That God does not give salvation except in a way of seeking, appears to be his general thesis which he preached insistently and repeatedly. " It is his (God's) will to give converting grace in the use of means, among which this is one, *viz.*, to lead a moral and religious life, and agreeable to our light, and the convictions of our consciences." (Dwight *Works,* Vol. VI, p. 312.) In a sermon on the prodigal son he considers the question why men should seek salvation. The first part of his fourfold answer is that God never bestows salvation until men seek it earnestly. In still another sermon he shows that it was necessary even in primitive times for men to seek salvation, although seeking took longer in the eighteenth century because of the increased wickedness of men. Conversions that come without seeking are usually not genuine. " Sudden conversions are very often false." (Matt. 13:5; sermon no. 4.) An easy way to salvation was suspect (Matt. 7:13-14) .

God has two reasons, at least, for stipulating seeking as the way of finding salvation. It is not because there is any merit in seeking, nor that it itself in any way disposes God to bestow the blessing sought, nor that it is any substitute for faith, by which alone men can be justified and are justified. Rather, it is because, first, men in their fallen condition are unable to believe, and, second, the gift of faith is so great a gift that there should be some demonstration of a real desire before it is bestowed.

First, then, inability is one reason that men must seek. Strangely enough, Edwards' doctrine of men's ability to seek for salvation is no proof that he believed in their ability to find salvation. This " seeking " doctrine is often thought to be an un-Calvinistic note in his preaching. If men are able to seek, it is said, they are able to find salvation. But this is a great *non sequitur,* according to Edwards. Because sinners are able to seek, it does not mean that, of themselves, they may be able to find. The two do not necessarily go together at all. But Edwards believed that if they sought, God might reveal to them the salvation that they sought — not because they sought it, but because he might choose to give it in such a circumstance as seeking.

Still, why should they seek at all, especially since by seeking they are not able to find? Why should they not simply believe and be saved? The answer for Edwards was that they were unable to believe. They had no disposition to believe; nor could they, in their fallen and sinful condition, ever have any disposition to believe. They were dead in trespasses and sins. The treatise on *The Great Christian Doctrine of Original Sin* is devoted to proving this. For Edwards, men were able to seek though they were not able to believe. And they were to seek precisely because they could not believe without the gift of faith from God which God would not give except in a way of seeking. Thus, instead of Edwards' doctrine of seeking implying ability, as so many think, it rested on the very opposite: inability. It was because men were unable to believe that they were to seek, not because they were able. They were able to seek, of course, but they were not able to believe. The Calvinistic doctrine of inability refers not to men's inability to seek, but to their inability to believe and/or to do any good.

Edwards was thoroughly Calvinistic in his doctrine.

God Makes Men Sensible (Hos. 5:15) is a sermon in which Edwards is concerned to show man's inability to believe and the necessity of his seeking if he is ever to receive ability. In it he shows the fallacy of those who think that believing is native to fallen man. Here is the manifest difference between the revivalism of Edwards and most of that which has characterized the last two centuries. A more modern evangelist would urge men to believe and would think that it was quite in man's power, in his pew or on his deathbed, to reach out and believe savingly. Usually such evangelists will regard all who, in response to such an invitation, do profess to believe as being saved then and there. They will usually count them as converts. Edwards thought no such thing. Belief was not in the sinners' dispositions. He told them so and warned them against thinking otherwise, especially in desperate circumstances when they realized that it was imperatively necessary that they believe and be saved.

Even with respect to seeking or striving, there was a right and a wrong way. Some strive to believe, and some strive to receive the gift of belief. There is a great difference between these two types of striving. One of them is presumptuous and can lead to no good eventuality. The other is acceptable to God even though the person who does so strive may himself be obnoxious to Him. Thus in the sermon on Gen. 3:24, discussing the sword that protected the Garden from the return of the ejected sinners, Edwards instructed his congregation that the sword still barred men from entering heaven who strove for it in their own name. Men must not strive to enter heaven, but strive to receive the gift of God by which alone they can be qualified to enter heaven.

The second reason for seeking salvation, even though that is a gift and not something to be earned by seeking or doing anything else, is that there is a certain propriety or fitness in being earnest about a gift so very great. It seemed to Edwards unsuitable for God to give this gift to men who had no interest at all in it. He is on dangerous ground here, if he would be consistent with his Calvinistic theology and avoid the Roman doctrine of a " merit of congruity." If men are altogether sinful, as he taught, their seeking would be utterly obnoxious, as he also taught, and there could hardly be any proportion between such seeking and such a gift, between the evil actions of men and the good gift of God. Edwards is fully aware of this danger and often speaks with reference to it. His solution is as follows: while it is true that all the actions of evil men, including seeking salvation, are evil, some are less evil than others. A fuller discussion of this matter will come later. Suffice it here to note that the " propriety " that Edwards finds between seeking and receiving the gift of salvation is not a true proportion or fitness, between the seeking and the gift, but a relative fitness or propriety. That is, the earnestness revealed by men in seeking is outwardly, but not inwardly, in keeping with the dignity of the gift for which they seek. On the other hand, if God gave this gift to those who did not seek, there would be nothing at all in the recipients that showed any disposedness to receive so great a gift.

" It becomes the wisdom of God so to order it that things of great value and importance should not be obtained without great labor and diligence." (Gen. 6:22.) And this principle applies to the matter of salvation. Seeking is not necessary to merit salvation, but it is necessary to prepare men for its reception.

Jan Ridderbos, in his *Theologie van Jonathan Edwards,* has this comment to make on Edwards' doctrine. Edwards' teaching on the will is so subtle " that in the popular mind it can make no other impression than that man's inability is relative.

This thought must be aroused when, for example, Edwards in one of his sermons (*The Manner of Seeking Salvation, Works,* Vol. II, p. 5), in the exhortation to seek salvation, urges upon both converted and unconverted that this is a very difficult work, but not something that is ' beyond the faculties of our nature, nor beyond the opportunities which God gives us so that each who is honest and earnest and uses all opportunities, shall not fail.' Added to this is the fact that Edwards calls the natural man less to conversion than to the preparations for conversion. This also is bound to weaken the perception that the natural man through preaching is called to do that which he shall never do unless the grace of God intervenes. All this makes it understandable that the theological development, to which he lent impetus, relatively quickly ran into that same Arminianism which he with so much energy had opposed." (Pages 138–139, translated by the Rev. H. Bajema in private correspondence with me.)

To this we must take exception. While we grant that Edwards' manner of speaking could have been misunderstood, there is no evidence that it was misunderstood. In his sermons, Edwards deals with many objections that his people raised from time to time, but never did he have to contend with those who were inclined to construe his words as implying their ability to save themselves or secure the gift of salvation. On the contrary, the opposite objection was the one that he was obliged to answer from time to time. The people must have wondered whether there was really any point in their doing anything, since God was absolutely sovereign and had already decreed all that was to come to pass, on the one hand, and they, on the other hand, were completely in bondage to evil and incapable of doing any good. As much as Edwards stressed the possibility of their seeking, they seem never to have gotten the impression that their seeking had any merit in it or would necessarily oblige God to save them. Indeed, when one considers the corpus of Edwards' sermons and finds passage after passage stressing the absolute dependence of men on God in the affair of redemption and, even in his many statements dealing with seeking, notes the care with which he defines his subject and wards off any possible misunderstanding, it is not at all surprising that the great opponent of Arminianism was never thought to have let Arminianism in by the back door.

As for the opinion that " the theological development, to which he (Edwards) lent impetus, relatively quickly ran into that same Arminianism which he with so much energy had opposed," we must deny it flatly. It is true, undeniably, that New England theology in another century had become Arminian and Pelagian, but this is by no means the same as saying that the theological movement to which Edwards gave impetus did so. His influence was all against this. Williston Walker, cited approvingly by B. B. Warfield in the *Hastings Encyclopedia of Religion and Ethics* (Vol. V, p. 226), rightly says that Edwards delayed " the elimination of Calvinism as a determining factor in the thought of New England " for a hundred years. The Arminianism that did come into vogue did so in spite of Edwards, not because of him. The Edwardeans were rightly called the consistent Calvinists. Samuel Hopkins, the great friend and biographer of Edwards, is an example in point. So far as this matter of the use of means is concerned, he perfectly perpetuated the tradition of his theological master. Joseph Haroutunian in his *Piety Versus Moralism* (pp. 57–58) observes that " Hopkins' solution to the problem was that means are necessary for the cultivation of godliness, but that they do not produce it." But then Professor Haroutunian goes on to say essentially the same thing about the teaching of Hopkins that Ridderbos has said about

Edwards'. " Of course, the distinction is somewhat subtle, and failed to carry conviction to the champions of striving." Granted, there is a degree of sublety here. It does not seem to be any more than the nature of the principle involved actually possesses. Hopkins could hardly have stated what he thought the Bible taught without such " subtlety." Nor could Edwards. If any of their followers were unable to make the necessary distinctions, Edwards and Hopkins, at least, could hardly be held responsible.

Directions for seeking salvation are found in almost every sermon Edwards ever preached. No theme was so much on his heart and lips as this. This was the point of contact between sinners and the gospel, and he was constantly urging it on them. Men were not able to believe, but they were able to seek, and so Edwards always was exhorting them to do so and telling them how to do it.

Speaking very generally, we may say that the directions that Edwards gives men for the mere seeking of salvation are more exacting than most evangelists give for the living of Christianity. In modern churches men whom Edwards regarded as merely seeking salvation would probably be pillars of the church and leading officers celebrated for their piety!

In the sermon on Mark 6:17-20, Edwards submits four reasons for men's failure in seeking even though they had done many things. To put it mildly, these reasons are puzzling. They are these: they did not hate sin as sin, did not count the cost, did not choose God for their whole portion, did not trust that God would reward their self-denials.

What is puzzling about this list is that two of them could not have characterized men as mere seekers. If they possessed qualities one and three (hating sin as sin and choosing God for their whole portion), they would not have been mere seekers, but finders. These are the marks of regenerate persons, and had they possessed them this would prove that fact. (We are aware that Edwards often represents Christians as seekers, but here he appears to be speaking of unregenerate seekers.) If their failure in these qualities doomed all their seeking, it would at the same time doom all seeking, for no mere seeker ever possessed them. The other two deficiencies (not counting the cost and not trusting that God would reward their self-denials) were possibly deficiencies in their natural ability. That is, they could have counted the cost, and from their self-interest alone been willing to meet it, and they could conceivably have trusted God's promise even though they did not love him. Still, there is a question about this last matter, for as we shall see, Edwards never taught men that they could assume that if they sought God, God would reward them with saving faith. It is a question, therefore, whether seekers could have had this trust, as seekers. Edwards tells them on other occasions that part of counting the cost is realizing that their efforts may be unavailing. God can rightly refuse all their efforts and may do so. How, then, could they have confident trust? And if they could not, how could this vitiate their seeking?

This raises the fundamental question concerning Edwards' doctrine of seeking. Is it possible that the qualities that he describes as constituting seeking, constitute a man a Christian? In this last passage we noted that he himself does list some things that he associates with seeking which clearly do not belong to mere seekers but to finders only. Is it possible that the sharp, analytical mind of Edwards is at this point somewhat blunted and he has run together in his thinking and preaching two things that should be kept separate: namely, qualities of mere seekers and of Christians themselves? Surely this is not true generally. For the most part he is very careful to distinguish between true religious affections and spurious ones, or those marks of conversion which cannot be approximated by the unconverted as well as those in which they are the same. That is to say, there are points where the lines do run together and points where they are sharply separate. Thus, for example, both seekers and finders must be violent, must practice universal obedience, must respect the Sabbath, etc., etc. Still, even with respect to these common things there are differences, not outwardly, but inwardly. In other words, true Christians do these things but from motives that differ from those of mere seekers. Unconverted seekers may do all these good things from the sinful motive of self-interest, while true Christians do the same things but from, partly at least, motives of love to God and man.

What we seem to have here is, therefore, an Edwardean inconsistency with his own doctrine. It is impossible for a natural man to hate sin as sin. It he did so, he would not be a natural, but a regenerate, man. Neither can he choose God as his whole portion, for this too is a mark of conversion. This inconsistency does not, however, invalidate the whole line of thought.

Edwards does not deny that men will be saved the moment that they believe. This he not only teaches, but he exhorts his hearers to believe and be saved. Prov. 28:13 is devoted to it, as is seen in the very doctrine: " God stands ready to forgive every sinner upon his hearty confessing and forsaking his sin." In support of this Edwards appeals to Ps. 32:5: " I acknowledged my sin unto thee, and mine iniquity have I not hid. I said, I will confess my transgressions unto the Lord; and thou forgavest the iniquity of my sin "; and to Isa. 55:7: " Let the wicked forsake his way, and the unrighteous man his thoughts: and let him return unto the Lord, and he will have mercy upon him; and to our God, for he will abundantly pardon."

Other sermons press the same truth. Thus, we find in
Ps. 25:11: " *If we truly come to God for mercy the greatness
of our sin will be no impediment to pardon* " (Dwight *Works,*
Vol. VI, p. 305) . In this sermon he shows the necessity of
coming from a sense of their misery and as beggars; and they
must come through Christ alone, acting upon his universal
offer of the gospel. In the application we find this encouragement: " Therefore if your souls be burdened and you are dis-
tressed for fear of hell, you need not bear that burden and
distress any longer. If you are but *willing* you may freely come
and unload yourselves and cast all your burdens on Christ
and rest in him. . . . If you can find it in your hearts to come
to Christ, and close with him, you will be accepted " (*ibid.,*
pp. 310, 312) .

One might suppose that men who sought salvation would
be willing to be made willing. This, however, is not the case.
To those who say that they would be glad to be made willing,
Edwards answers: No, you are not sincere in saying this, or
you would be willing. You are only afraid of hell, not desirous
of heaven. So we have the situation of persons seeking to be
made willing who are not, when they seek, willing to be made
willing! The position is not as strange as it at first sounds; nor
is it inconsistent with what Edwards has been saying all along.
Men in their fallen condition are not willing to do God's will.
And if they are not willing to do God's will, they are not
willing to be made willing, because this would be the same
thing as to say, contrary to the hypothesis, that they are willing. For being willing to be made willing and being willing
are equivalent. So when men begin to seek, they are seeking
to be made willing; but they are not willing to be made willing. Indeed, if they were willing to be made willing, they
would not need to seek to be made willing; they would be
willing before they began to seek. When, therefore, they seek

to be made willing, they are merely placing themselves where
God may make them willing. They have no disposition to this
at the outset, but they are willing to be given a disposition
because they are afraid of what will happen to them if this
disposition is not given to them.

At this point, the imaginary objector retorts that he would
be willing if God made him so, if God gave him grace. This
is presented as something of an indictment of God for not
giving him the grace to desire grace. Although Edwards has
just shown him that the sinner is not willing to be made willing, the sinner tries now to blame God for not making him
willing to be willing. To this, Edwards replies, " 'Tis no excuse of your wickedness that God han't hindered you from
being wicked." That is, you are to blame for not being willing
although only God can make you willing. Because God alone
can hinder the evil of your heart, it is nonetheless from your
heart and will that the evil comes. Furthermore, Edwards
continues, your heart has wickedly abused what assistance it
has had.

While there is a difference in the way in which Christians
seek and natural men seek, each group is to continue doing
it. There is no ground for Christians thinking that because
they have found God they are thereafter to cease seeking for
him. You are, says Edwards, to seek the spiritual manna as
laboriously as if you had never found it (Ex. 16:20). Likewise, converted men as well as unconverted need to be converted (Luke 22:32). They must reform themselves thoroughly (Matt. 11:12), striving against every expression of
their native corruption (Luke 17:16), going as far as they are
naturally able (Matt. 7:13-14), practicing universal obedience (Num. 23:20), conforming themselves to all duty (Luke
16:16), being careful not to offend (Hos. 11:3) or mock God
(Jer. 5:31). They are to search the Bible and examine them-

selves in its light (Matt. 11:12). They are to submit themselves to God, especially to his sovereignty (Jer. 8:11), and to pray and wrestle with him desperately (Matt. 11:12; Luke 19:10; Gen. 32:26), especially at times when he is near (Hos. 11:3).

Edwards makes this quality of seeking the first characteristic of the apostle Paul in the revival sermon preached in February, 1740, on *The Character of Paul an Example to Christians* (Phil. 3:17). " The apostle did not only thus earnestly seek salvation before his conversion and hope, but afterwards [also]. What he says in the third [chapter] of Philippians of his suffering the loss of all things, that he might be found in Christ, and its being the one thing that he did to seek salvation; and also what he says of his so running as not uncertainly, but as resolving to win the prize of salvation, and keeping under his body that he might not be a castaway; was long after his conversion and after he had received his hope of his own good estate.

" If being already converted excuses a man from seeking salvation any more, or makes it reasonable that he should leave off his earnest care and labour for it, certainly the apostle might have been excused, when he had not only already attained true grace, but such eminent degrees of it. To see one of the most eminent saints that ever lived [or, laboured?] if not [the] very eminentest of all, so exceedingly engaged in seeking his own salvation — it ought for ever to put to shame those that are a thousand degrees below him, and are but mere infants to him, if they have any grace at all; that yet excuse themselves from using any violence after the kingdom of heaven now, because they have attained already, easing themselves of the burden of going on earnestly to seek salvation with this, that they have got through the work, they have got a hope.

" The apostle, as eminent as he was, did not say within himself, ' I am converted, and so am sure of salvation. Christ has promised it me; What need I care any further about obtaining salvation? Yea, I am not only converted, but I have obtained great degrees of grace.' . . . The apostle knew that though he was converted, yet there remained a great work that he must do, in order to his salvation. There was a narrow way to eternal glory, that he must pass through and never could come to the crown of glory any other way. He knew that it was absolutely necessary for him earnestly to seek salvation still; he knew there was no going to heaven in a lazy way.

" And therefore he did not seek salvation the less earnestly, for his having hope, yea, and assurance, but a great deal more. We nowhere read so much of his earnestness and violence for the kingdom of heaven before he was converted as we do afterwards. . . .

" Most certainly if the apostle was in the right way of acting, we in this place are generally in the wrong. For nothing is more apparent than that it is not thus with the generality of professors but that 'tis a common thing after they think they are safe, to be abundantly less diligent and earnest in religion than before."

The ways in which a man is to seek salvation are virtually innumerable. In one sermon Edwards gives seventeen directions, in another fourteen (Luke 15:16), and many more in many other sermons. The corpus of his sermons include about every known external duty as a proper preparation for salvation or a method of seeking it. Thus, be prepared to leave your country (Num. 23:20), seek for salvation as for hidden treasure (Matt. 2:10), cultivate all moral and religious duties, including the attendance at private meetings (Rom. 11:7). Counting the cost is often said to be a way of seeking, and the seeker is at the same time reminded that he must bear in mind that though he count the cost and be willing to pay he cannot count on his seeking being successful. Indeed, realizing that the seeking may not be fruitful seems to be part of counting the cost (Luke 16:16; Matt. 11:12). Seekers must wait on God (Num. 23:20; Isa. 40:31), trust only in Christ (Jer. 8:11). But while waiting they must be very active in doing (Matt. 11:12), be prepared to sell all (Gen. 6:22), persist in spite of many difficulties and dangers (Jer. 8:11; Job 32:20) without weariness (Jer. 5:31). They must act immediately (Job 32:20) and violently (Luke 18:38; I Cor. 9:26), improving every day as the last (Deut. 32:35).

Prayer deserves special attention in the discussion of seeking. It would seem to present a problem in the Edwardean scheme. Why does he exhort men to pray who have no disposition to worship God sincerely? On the surface of it this would appear to be an invitation to hypocrisy. We have here the same problem that we have faced with respect to seeking in general. This is but a specific instance of it. The problem is this: Why, if men have no disposition to seek God sincerely or pray to God sincerely, should they be exhorted by a messenger of God to pray? As we shall now see, Edwards' answer to this specific problem is in the same terms as those with which he answers the general problem.

First of all, he declares prayer to be a universal duty. All men should pray, he says in a sermon on Neh. 1:3-4. Nature teaches this, man's dependence on God shows it, and, furthermore, God has commanded it. Natural men should pray for communion with God (Ps. 10:17).

Still, while it is a duty for all men to pray, fallen men are no more able to perform this duty than they are able to repent and believe the gospel, which they are also commanded to do. " The true spirit of prayer is no other than God's own

Spirit dwelling in the hearts of the saints. That being a Spirit that comes from God, does naturally tend to God in holy breathings [and] pantings . . . therefore the Spirit is said to make intercessions (Job 27:10) . . . . True prayer is nothing else but faith expressed. Hence we read of the prayer of faith, Jas. 5:15. True Christian prayer is the faith and reliance of the soul breathed forth in words." It is perfectly clear from this that no natural man is able so to pray. He does not have the Spirit of God dwelling in him, nor does he have the principle of faith. There is no " holy panting " of his soul after God. Edwards says positively, citing Hos. 7:14 in proof, that evil men do not pray, for prayer is a talking of children to their Father (Ps. 66:18).

In spite of this, Edwards urges sinners to pray and to pray fervently. As usual he is aware of the problem and speaks to it. Yes, he acknowledges, for a natural man to pray would be for an enemy of God to attempt to commune with him. But this is not wrong. There is nothing inconsistent with praying earnestly with mortal hatred in the heart or the highest pride, Isa. 14:12 (Luke 8:28). Such prayer would not be virtuous or even true prayer, but it would avoid a more willful act of disobedience. It is better, Edwards argues, to " pray out of self love than neglect prayer out of self love." Such prayer is " materially evil but formally good "; the omission of it would be " both materially and formally evil." He finds support for his position by an analogy. Thus he appeals to the Epistle of James in which it is said that wicked men believe in God. James approves, saying, " Thou doest well." The way in which wicked men believe is wicked, not good; yet they are said to do well. This means that the act of belief itself is good although the heart from which the profession comes is not. Similarly, prayer may be good although the pray-er may not be. It is better to perform a duty from an evil motive than not to perform it from an evil motive. There is more sin in lying to gratify a lust than in telling the truth to gratify a lust. It is better for evil men to save a drowning person than not to save him.

The question arises, of course, whether prayer, in this sense of the word, is a duty. Is this what God commanded? Did he ask men to come before him in this manner, or did he command true prayer? Edwards has shown that true prayer is the panting of a devout heart after God. If this is commanded, is the mere form of this exercise in any sense a response to this command? Is it possibly a mockery of it, worse than no response at all? We do not find Edwards facing up to this particular objection, nor can we surmise what he would say to it on his principles.

But he does say that wicked men should pray and, among other things, they should pray that their wickedness be brought home to their consciousness. Pray, he says, that God may " discover " your heart to you (Matt. 10:17) . Again, an ungracious person should pray to have his heart made sensible of its need of grace (Rom. 9:31) .

Edwards assures sinners that the prayers that proceed from their wicked hearts so hostile to God may be the occasion of his pity. Of course, the prayers themselves could never be the cause of the divine pity, for they are obnoxious in themselves. " There is no goodness in praying though it be never so earnestly merely out of a fear of misery " (Luke 8:28) . But God may pity them and answer in grace, rather in spite of than because of the prayers; very much as he may give faith to those who seek without a desire in their heart for what they seek. This is God's appointed way to pardon (Luke 8:28) . Prayer may begin on an evil principle and end on a good one. In spite of the wickedness of the hearts of devils and fallen men, God sometimes hears them. He does so not out of regard to their self-interest, but only as he is pleased to hear the voice of nature — as he hears the voice of the ravens. Thus he listened to wicked King Ahab in I Kings 21:20 (Ps. 66:18). If natural men are commanded to pray to be made sensible of their need of grace, God does sometimes use this very means to make them sensible and dependent and thus he prepares them, according to Ezek. 23:39, to receive the grace that he is disposed to give to them. As a matter of fact, God ordinarily gives blessing in answer to prayer (Gen. 32:26). Some seekers he tests by making them wrestle with him in prayer. Thus Edwards apparently applies the experience of Jacob wrestling with the " angel," which seems to have been the experience of a converted soul, to the experience of the unconverted.

CHAPTER

X

ABLE BUT NOT WILLING

A LL MEN, except the committers of the unpardonable sin, have a " chance " or " opportunity " to be saved. While there is temporal life there is hope of eternal life, so far as men, who do not know the decrees of God, are concerned. As early as 1733, Edwards is preaching that " persons ought to do what they can for their salvation " (Eccl. 9:10) . In an even earlier sermon (Eccl. 4:5; Andover) we find him arguing the case: " 'Tis true men never will be disposed to use the means unless they are awakened . . . but that don't argue that the using the means is not in their power." Men can perform no human action till they are first made willing, and they won't be willing unless they judge it needful and in some way for their benefit, but this does not argue that they have no natural power to do it. " The reason why they don't use the means is not because they could not if they were disposed but because they are not disposed." Furthermore, our evangelist concludes, men not only have the power but the necessary principles as well.

During the first revival Edwards preached the same doctrine. " If men be but sensible of the need of it they ordinarily have it in their power to take likely methods in order to their salvation." (Ezek. 33:4-5.) He lists six things that unconverted men can do and then gives three arguments to show they have this much ability. First, it is implicit in the appointment of means of grace. Second, men are condemned for their inconsiderateness and slothfulness, and this presupposes power to do otherwise. Third, God encourages the use of means which he would not do if men were unable to use them.

In the great revival of the early forties Edwards is still preaching this ability. Exhorting, he says: " Some have now no opportunity to seek it (light) and find. Their opportunity is past. But 'tis not so with you. You have full opportunity, a blessed opportunity; if you can but find it in your heart to improve it as you may do " (Matt. 2:10) . In his famous sermon on *Pressing Into the Kingdom* we read these words: " So there is no want either of sufficiency in God, or capacity in the sinner, in order to this." And later: " Though earnestness of mind be not immediately in your power, yet the consideration of what has been now said of the need of it, may be a means of stirring you up to it. . . . The dullness and deadness of the heart, and slothfulness of disposition, don't hinder men's being *able* to take pains; tho' it hinders their being willing." (*Discourses on Various Important Subjects,* pp. 142–144.) By this last statement, Edwards does not mean that men are hindered from being willing to take pains, but from being willing to be saved. This is another statement of the theme that we noted above: men may will to seek salvation though they do not will to be saved.

In a sermon delivered when the ordeal with his congregation was beginning to take shape, Edwards gives an interesting analogy to his doctrine. " The means of grace to those that live under the gospel are like the showers that often descend on the earth." (Heb. 6:7.) In this he compares fallen man to the earth which has no principle of fruitfulness but has a capacity for it. Just as the earth does not have the seed in itself but can receive it, so the sinner is devoid of the principle of life but can receive it. This is what Edwards means, clearly stated, by capacity or ability. Again: " God's blessing is attainable. There is a possibility of being delivered from our natural state and obtaining those supernatural qualifications that are spoken of . . . ," he insists in the sermon on Num. 23:20.

Edwards continued this doctrine to the end of his ministry. In a Stockbridge sermon of 1754, he laments that the greater part of those who live under the gospel, as well as others, perish (Job 32:20). Still, he goes on, they have the opportunity to escape; they can hope if they hurry; they may arrive at a remarkable happiness in the end. Then he gives five directions for seekers.

As late as 1757 he was saying of Dives, who had gone to hell, that he had had a " fair opportunity " (Luke 16:25). God had " waited to be gracious." Indeed, Dives had had a better opportunity than many who obtained salvation.

There is a significant connection between the inability of sinners and their ability. In Edwards' thinking it is the realization of their moral inability that is the occasion for the realization of and exercise of their natural ability. The sinner may object, as Edwards represents him in the sermon on Luke 16:16, that the strong desire for salvation that he needs is quite out of his reach. True, replies Edwards, but the need of it may stir you up to seek it. If you will use the means that are within your reach, God may give you what is not in your reach. To be sure, some things are beyond their present disposition, he went on, but they are not beyond fallen men's capacity.

As we have already observed, many interpreters of Edwards think that his insistence on seeking and opportunity and possibility of salvation, and the like, implied that he believed in

the ability of man, rather than the Calvinistic doctrine of inability. It should be clear from the above that this is not the
case. No one ever preached depravity and moral inability
more thoroughly than Edwards. And, as has been said, it was
that doctrine which was to lead sinners to do what they could.
Since they could not do what was immediately necessary,
namely, believe and be saved, let them do what they could do
for themselves, namely, seek.

A comparison, at this point, of the preaching of Edwards
and his great English contemporary John Wesley is enlightening. On the surface, their similarities are striking. Each
preached the gospel of grace, commanded men everywhere to
repent, and taught that justification was by faith alone. Each
was an " experimental " preacher, that is, he preached the
necessity of men's experiencing the truths of Christianity.
They were " affectionate " preachers, believing that the affections, no less but more than the mind, must be moved in
true conversion. Each believed that the majority, even of professing Christians, were merely nominal and few would be
saved. Each was an outstanding leader in the Awakening in
his country. And, so far as their acquaintance permitted, each
had respect for the other. We know that John Wesley read
The Narrative of Surprising Conversions and, in an edited
form, had it published in England. Edwards, in one of his sermons preached at a private meeting, December, 1739, mentions Wesley as a man of whom he has heard and of whom he
approves so far as he is familiar with his work (II Cor. 8:1) .

There is another similarity between the two men which
also contains their major differences as well. Each wrote a
refutation of John Taylor's *Doctrine of Original Sin*. Wesley's
*The Doctrine of Original Sin (The Works of the Rev. John
Wesley,* 3d edition, Vol. IX, pp. 191 ff.) appeared in 1756.
Edwards' *The Great Christian Doctrine of Original Sin* was

going through the presses in the year he died, 1758. Each man was aroused by Taylor's Pelagian denial of the traditional doctrine. Incidentally, each man had Taylor's book put in his hands by a friend. In their main battle lines they take common ground against a common foe. Edwards' position is more philosophical and profound than Wesley's, but their adherence to the Biblical doctrine of the fall is common.

The great difference between the two men in their books on original sin explains the divergence in their preaching. It runs, as something of a refrain, through Wesley's book that although man had fallen in sin because of his own disobedience and although he was now justly exposed to condemnation, God was obliged to give him a chance to be saved. " The state of mankind did so far depend on Adam, that, by his fall, they all fell into sorrow, and pain, and death, spiritual and temporal. And all *this is noways inconsistent with either the justice or goodness of God, provided all may recover through the Second Adam, whatever they lost through the first; nay, and recover it with unspeakable gain . . .* " (*The Works of the Rev. John Wesley,* p. 332) (italics ours). Thus it becomes a matter not of grace, but of law, that God provide a gospel. It is not merely that God would be unmerciful if he deprived men of a chance to be saved, but Wesley infers that he would be unjust as well. In spite of the fact that Wesley represents man as having fallen because of his own sin, for which he alone was to blame, and in spite of the fact that man left to himself would justly perish, Wesley goes on to insist that God has an obligation to give him an opportunity to be delivered from the predicament into which he alone has brought himself. Wesley apparently never saw any illogicality in this. The characteristic Wesleyan doctrine, that Christ by his death has given men the ability to believe by which (if they refuse to exercise it) they are justly condemned to hell, follows from this position taken in Wesley's *Original Sin*.

There is no such doctrine in Edwards' book. When angels sinned they were plunged into condemnation immediately, without offer or hope of deliverance. Such was the just decree of God. It would have been equally just with God to have done the same with mankind when it fell. He had no obligation to do otherwise. Innumerable sermons enunciate this doctrine, and I have never seen anything inconsistent with it in all the writings of Edwards. But rather than citing these abundant sources, we will appeal to a sermon in which he shows that even if men had not sinned, God would have had no obligation to offer them eternal life. The manuscript sermon on Luke 17:9 develops this fully. Its doctrine is: " God don't thank men for doing those things which he commands them."

There are three significant differences in the salvation theory of Edwards and Wesley which appear to have had far-reaching repercussions on their preaching. First, Wesley affirmed and Edwards denied that God had an obligation to offer salvation to sinful man. This difference not only altered their conception of grace itself in a fundamental manner, but it accounts largely for their characteristic Arminianism and Calvinism. That is to say, it was because Wesley believed that God had an obligation to give all fallen men a chance, in the fullest sense of the word, to believe and be saved that he necessarily and vigorously repudiated the doctrine of election. On the other hand, Edwards' doctrine of election, which he preached with the fervor that Wesley denied it, was perfectly consistent with his view of sin and grace.

The second great difference was on the matter of fallen man's ability to believe and be saved. Wesley maintained this as a necessary corollary to his conviction that God was under obligation to give men an opportunity to be saved, in the ultimate sense of the word opportunity. If God were thus obliged, he would do what he was obliged to do: namely, give fallen men the full ability to believe and be saved. This he did give and this Wesley preached to fallen sinners as their birthright. Sinners " have all, then, a natural propensity to sin. Nevertheless, this propensity is not necessary, if by necessary you mean irresistible. We can resist and conquer it too, by the grace which is ever at hand." (*Op. cit.*, p. 294.) Edwards, on the other hand, denied categorically that men had any such ability and he preached their inability. As we have seen, he made this very inability the basis of their seeking for ability.

The third difference bears most immediately on the preaching of Wesley and Edwards. Since one man thought that sinners had moral ability and the other did not, the appeal to these sinners was, of course, vastly different. Wesley always preached for decision. He appealed to men to believe and be saved, confidently assured that they were able to respond favorably to his invitation. Edwards, however, urged men to do far differently. He would not usually call upon them to believe and be saved (though he did do this; cf. the sermon on Rev. 3:20 which exhorts to belief without any mention of seeking) because that was not in the realm of their ability, but called them to *seek* to be enabled to believe and be saved because that was in the realm of their ability.

Chapter XI

ENCOURAGEMENT FOR RELUCTANT
SEEKERS

IN SPITE of all his fiery warnings, strong doctrine of reprobation, teaching that few would be saved, and stressing the
bondage of sin, Jonathan Edwards was a reassuring and even
an encouraging evangelist. As a matter of fact, the only question is how encouraging he is. That he is most optimistic
about the outcome of genuine seeking there can be no question; the question is how optimistic is he.

I examined fifty or more sermons that dealt with this subject to see the general tenor of his preaching about the outcome of seeking for salvation. To get some impression of his
teaching and emphasis I checked these sermons, trying to discover whether they indicated that the outcome would be uncertain, possibly successful, probably successful, or certainly
successful. Of these sermons, twenty-seven were clear in their
answers to our question. Of these, I found that twelve taught
that the sinner would probably be successful in his seeking,
seven that he would possibly be successful, five that the outcome was uncertain, and three that the seeker would certainly
find, if some specific conditions were met. There is a problem here, obviously, with the category of the " certain." If
the outcome of seeking is certain to be successful, it could not
be uncertain, clearly; but neither could it be merely possible

or even merely probable. It could, if uncertain, be possible or even probable; but if certain, these other categories would appear to be ruled out. We shall face up to this problem shortly, but first let us get some feel of Edwards' teaching on the subject by considering some of these statements briefly.

The predominant teaching of Edwards seems to be that men will probably succeed if they seek properly. Thus, in his revival sermon *Pressing Into the Kingdom* we have these words: " He that is diligent and *painful* in all duty, probably won't be *so* long, before he finds the *sensibleness* of his heart, and *earnestness* of his spirit greatly increased " (*Discourses on Various Important Subjects*, p. 145) . The following statement in the same sermon is plainer and unmistakable: " If you sit still you die, if you go backward behold you shall surely die, if you go forward you may live. And though God has not bound himself to any thing that a person does, while destitute of faith, and out of Christ, yet there is great probability, that in a way of hearkening to this counsel, you *will live* " (*ibid.*, p. 153) . In the same year he said in another message: " If you behave yourself in seeking heaven in the manner that has been spoken there is good reason to think God will help you " (Matt. 11:12) ; and also these words: " If you seek it as you may do there is great hope that you may find it " (Matt. 2:10) . In a sermon on divine sovereignty preached during the first revival we find him saying that sovereignty does not deny that those most careful are most likely to obtain (John 3:8) . In a still earlier sermon he had said: " The success and blessing depends on free grace and the sovereign pleasure of God but we don't want encouragement in the Word of God to be diligent in the use of means. When persons do what they can God usually does that for them that is not in their own power." (Eccl. 4:5; Andover.) In the interim between the revivals he preached this doctrine cited above: " If men be but sensible of the need of it they ordinarily have it in their power to take likely methods in order to their salvation " (Ezek. 33:4-5). Encouraging men to pray, as Jacob prayed to the angel to bless him, Edwards assured them that ordinarily God gives blessing in answer to prayer (Gen. 32:26). In his *Natural Men in a Dreadful Condition* (Acts 16:29-30) he declares that " it is a very rare thing, that ever any that are thoroughly in earnest for salvation and are so perseveringly that fail of salvation, unless they have put off the work until they were near death before they began." Even those who have forsaken God when they " come to seek him so as to search for him with all their hearts they are in the way to find him " (Jer. 29:13). As late as the last year of his Northampton ministry he is encouraging sinners to seek salvation (Jer. 50:4-5). And in the Rom. 3:11 sermon he says: " God is pleased commonly to bestow his saving grace on those that diligently and constantly? seek it in an attendance on those duties that are materially right though formally wrong and sinful."

The tone of other exhortations, while still encouraging, is not nearly so much so as those above. " God's blessing is attainable. That there is a possibility of being delivered from our natural state is the much more modest statement of the sermon on Num. 23:20, preached in 1746, on which we commented above. In a revival sermon of 1741 he is content to say that God sometimes hears the prayers of natural men, not always or even most of the time (Mark 2:17). The same sentiment is expressed in the sermon on Ps. 66:18.

Probably the most interesting treatment of this theme is in the very early sermon on II Kings 7:3-4. Edwards shows the reasonableness of seeking without guarantee of success. The Scripture tells of the leprous beggars who sat at the gates of besieged and famine-ridden Samaria while the Syrian army was encamped nearby. The lepers were faced with the problem of going within the gates and dying of starvation or venturing into the Syrian camp whereby they would run the risk of death but also had a chance of being spared. They wisely decided to venture into the enemy camp. Finding it abandoned, they were able to take the spoils left behind. The spiritual parallel that Edwards deduces from this incident becomes the doctrine of his sermon. " A possibility of being saved is much to be preferred to a certainty of perishing." He first indicates five ways in which there is a certainty of perishing: neglecting our souls; continuing in any way of known sin; becoming discouraged in seeking salvation; continuing to trust in our own righteousness; and quarreling with God, especially with his decrees. He next shows that there is a possibility of salvation for all except committers of the unpardonable sin, even for those who have been very great sinners and for those who are very old and still unconverted. The third part of the sermon is a consideration of the reasons of the doctrine, or why " a possibility of being saved is much to be preferred to a certainty of perishing." First, final destruction is so dreadful that all difficulties undergone in seeking salvation are worth it on the mere chance of being successful. Any calamity whatever is worth enduring if there is the least possibility of avoiding the ultimate calamity. A thousand times more pain than is ever felt in this world is justified by the mere possibility of salvation. Second, eternal life is a thing so desirable that the least hope of obtaining it outweighs any difficulties incurred in gaining it. Even if there were no hell, it would be worth every suffering to inherit heaven.

Some statements of Edwards' not only affirm the uncertainty of the outcome of seeking, but make an important point of it. That is, the sovereignty of God and the due humility of men seem to require that the seeking be done without guarantee of success. Thus Edwards likens seekers to soldiers set to take a city, but not knowing in advance whether they will succeed in their attempt or not (Matt. 11:12). People, when they seek sincerely, should be willing to be unassured in advance (*Natural Men in a Dreadful Condition,* Acts 16:29-30). Even more to this point is Edwards' frequent statement that some who seek, and who seek earnestly, do not find (Mark 10:17 f.; Rom. 11:7). The doctrine of the sermon on Rom. 11:7, a 1740 revival sermon, is: "There are multitudes of men that seek for salvation that never obtain what they seek for."

Encouraging as Edwards was, he didn't guarantee that seekers would necessarily have success. I was puzzled at first by a statement in the published sermon on Gen. 6:22 that "they shall succeed," which was a guarantee. However, when I examined the manuscript I discovered that not Edwards but the editor had written these words. The sentence Edwards actually wrote, and no doubt preached, was as follows: "If men will but take warning and will hearken to counsel, and will but be in good earnest, will be seasonable in their work, will take their opportunities — improve their advantages — follow the best advice — be steadfast and not wavering; *they are not wont to fail*" (italics ours). On the other hand, Edwards admits that some had sought salvation for twenty years without finding. Nevertheless, he insisted that they had sought with a "slack hand" (Prov. 26:11). In a sermon on Prov. 27:1, Edwards tells his hearers that when they seek they must expect or hope to find.

Likewise Edwards preached that if men sought for the Kingdom of God with as much zeal as they strove for worldly wealth, they would find salvation. This is not saying that men will thus seek; it even seems to imply that men do not so seek. But it says, nonetheless, that if men, even natural and sinful men, sought with that degree of earnestness, which seems clearly within their natural power, they would succeed. We cannot say, however, that this passage really teaches the certainty of success for all seekers, but only for some. But it does say this much: the right kind of seeking will certainly issue in salvation.

If we try to co-ordinate the certainty doctrine of Jonathan Edwards and its bearing on his other teachings, we come to something like the following. First, he certainly does not say that all seeking shall be successful, that all who seek, even seriously, shall find. Second, he does teach that all who seek as earnestly as they seek for worldly honor and glory shall succeed. Third, to be consistent with this, his uncertainty doctrine (that seekers must recognize at the outset of their search that the issue is uncertain and entirely dependent on the undeclared will of God) would have to mean that it is uncertain whether a given seeker would have sufficient seriousness of purpose and, therefore, it would be uncertain what the outcome would be. Fourth, to be consistent with the above certainty doctrine, Edwards' statements on possibility and probability would have to mean this: that if men once begin to seek, it is possible and even probable that they will become sufficiently serious and therefore will certainly find. This seems to me to be the consistent view of these different teachings; but at the same time I feel definitely that that is not what Edwards meant to say. I think he meant to say that any serious seeking would probably issue in salvation. But in that case, what are we to make of his statement that it shall certainly succeed? One of two things: either a plain inconsistency (something to which Edwards was by no means addicted) ; or, that serious seeking in general would probably be successful, while this specially serious seeking (that which was more zealous than the search for worldly glory) would certainly succeed.

No matter how great past sins have been, God is willing to forgive them. *" If we truly come to God for mercy, the greatness of our sin will be no impediment to pardon."* (Dwight *Works,* Vol. VI, p. 305.) It is as easy for God to forgive a great sin as a small one, for after all, that mercy " which is infinite, is as much above what is great, as it is above what is small." No one has anything of value to offer to God. " You can never come to Christ at all, unless you first see that he will not accept of you the more readily for any thing that you can do." Such doctrine was at once a blow to the self-righteous and an encouragement to those by sin oppressed.

There is even encouragement for those who have backslidden and sinned grossly and may be aged sinners. How ever much their possibility of being saved is diminished by these things, and though it becomes increasingly improbable that they ever will find, there is always hope for all who have not actually committed the unpardonable sin (Jer. 29:13).

Edwards is not only encouraging to seekers, but he seems even indulgent. He stresses the smallness of the necessary effort in comparison to the infinite value of the gift involved. Insistent as he is on earnest strivings, self-denial, and willingness to be violent, he declared that these are nothing in comparison to the reward offered.

CHAPTER
XII

PROPITIOUS TIMES FOR SEEKING

SEEKING for salvation should be done now, immediately, whatever may be the circumstances. But there are times that are especially propitious for successful seeking. These should be "improved" by any persons needing salvation. These red-letter days for redemption are times when God manifests his saving presence in an especial measure. It is a "blessed time amongst a people when it is a time of the pouring out of God's Spirit upon them" (Acts 8:8), and the people are exhorted to pray for such times and for the ministers God is wont to use. In a sermon on Matt. 7:13, preached during the great revival in 1740, Edwards gives directions for entering at the strait gate. His exhortation is urgent, for at that time God appeared ready to help sinners and they should make the most of his willingness, since his help is absolutely necessary. Later in the same year Edwards speaks of the propitiousness of these times.

He reflects in 1746, after the great revival was long past, that "sinners are oftentimes converted in great numbers at a time" of special pouring out of the Spirit (Matt. 13:47-50). Such times are jubilee periods in which spiritual slaves should seek their liberation. As people see so many being saved, they should go along with them to the Holy Land as Ruth leaving

Moab went with her mother-in-law to Bethlehem (Ruth
1:16; also, cf. the sermon on Hos. 5:15). Such periods of revival are periods of God's special presence, and only fools will
fail to take advantage of their unusual opportunity. " They
that don't observe and improve their special seasons for the
good of their souls are less observant (?) of what is for their
own preservation and comfort than the very fowls of the air."
(Jer. 8:7.)

Because these periods are so full of hope for the unsaved,
failure to take advantage of them leads to most serious consequences. " When the Spirit of God has been remarkably
poured out in his converting and saving influences on a people 'tis an awful thing to dwell among them and yet have no
part nor lot in the matter." (Acts 8:21.) Men usually perish
after a day of grace which they have not utilized (Luke
19:44); because it is difficult to get into the Kingdom even
in these times and more so afterward (Mark 8:38). " If
sinners ? their day of grace they will surely perish." Thus
Jerusalem was given up to judicial blindness when it rejected
Christ in those days of great revival. If ever those that are far
from conversion are to be converted, it must be in a time
when God is near. If they miss this, commonly they go to hell
(Luke 19:42). " Those that sin away their day of grace shall
be wholly cast away by God as to any regard to their welfare."
(Prov. 1:26-27.)

Perhaps Edwards' most comprehensive statement on this
subject was made in the revival sermon *Pressing Into the
Kingdom* (Luke 16:16). " God hath his certain days, or appointed seasons of the exercise both of mercy and judgment.
There are some seasons that are remarkable times of wrath,
that are laid out by God for that purpose, *viz.*, for his awful
visitation, and the executions of his anger; which times are
called days of vengeance, Prov. 6. 34, and days wherein God

will visit for sin, Exod. 32.34. And so on the contrary, there are some other times, that God has laid out in his sovereign counsels, for seasons of remarkable mercy, wherein he will appear, and manifest himself, in the exercises of his grace and loving-kindness, more than at other times: Such times, in Scripture are called by way of eminency, accepted times, and days of salvation, and also days of God's visitation; because they are days wherein God will visit in a way of mercy; as Luke 19. 44. . . . 'Tis such a time now in this town; . . . It is indeed a *day of grace* with us as long as we live in this world, in the enjoyment of the *means of grace;* but such a time as this, is especially, and in a distinguishing manner, a day of grace . . . when *conversion* and *salvation* work is going on amongst us from Sabbath to Sabbath . . ." (*Discourses on Various Important Subjects,* 1738, pp. 154–155.)

God was wont to humble a seeker before he exalted him to salvation. Edwards often spoke of the " wilderness " experience or humbling that usually preceded deliverance. This is the theme of the sermon on Hos. 2:15. In the context God is threatening Israel because of her adultery. These threatenings came upon her in the fall and captivity in Assyria. But in the fourteenth verse God's gracious promise of mercy is announced. He gives Israel a bill of divorce in v. 2 but will make her his wife again in vs. 16, 19, 20. Then he shows how he will allure her. He will bring her into the wilderness to humble her and then will court her as a young man courts a maid. So God first shows hope and then he brings Israel into the humbling of the wilderness that she may realize that these good things come from him and not from her lovers. He then turns the wilderness into a vineyard. From this Edwards formulates the doctrine: " God is wont to cause hope and comfort to arise to souls after trouble and humbling for sin, and according as the troubler's slain and forsaken " (Hos.

2:15; Andover) . In an earlier sermon he draws the same lesson from the experience of Jonah: " There is encouragement for persons that have been seeking mercy though they are under never so dark and discouraging circumstances yet to look again toward God's holy temple " (Jonah 2:4) . In still another sermon he addresses the awakened, urging them not to be discouraged, but on the contrary to seek to be convinced that they are in this wilderness in which hope will spring up (Deut. 32:13) . In the great revival sermon on Gen. 6:22 he says: " Some are almost driven to despair " before comfort comes, and even after this comfort does come, are afterward again involved in darkness.

The great danger against which he warns those in the wilderness is a discouragement that leads to melancholy. There is perhaps nothing in the world, according to the sermon on II Cor. 13:5, that Satan makes a greater handle of than the disease of melancholy. Edwards could never forget his uncle, Joseph Hawley, who, because of the melancholy that developed from his experiences during the early revival, committed suicide. The pathetic funeral sermon Edwards preached on the occasion carried this doctrine: " We are all in ourselves utterly without any strength or power to help ourselves " (Rom. 5:6) .

The " propitious times " referred to in this section are, of course, special times or seasons of revival of an unscheduled or unpredictable character. There was also, however, one regularly recurring occasion that held special significance and potentiality for blessing. That was the administration of the Lord's Supper. For most of his preaching ministry, Edwards seems to have tacitly agreed with Solomon Stoddard's doctrine of the Eucharist as a " converting ordinance." That is not to say that he thought that this Sacrament had any *ex opere operato* tendency in itself to convert the person who observed

it — but neither did Stoddard think so. Stoddard would be
in agreement with Edwards' reminder that the people were
not to use means of grace " thinking that there is any merit
or natural efficacy in the means but only as an appointed way
of waiting on a sovereign God " (John 3:8). That 1734 (?)
statement shows at once that Edwards thought it a duty to
wait on God although he was utterly sovereign in bestowing
or withholding grace. And there was something of a calcu-
lated risk in the use of means of grace, for if God does not
bless them, they will stir up corruption (Isa. 1:5). " The same
means of grace are attended with a quite diverse and contrary
influence and consequence on different persons." (Micah
5:7-8.)

The duty of using the Sacrament in seeking salvation is
made very clear in the undated sermon on Prov. 8:34. Its
doctrine is: " The way to obtain grace is daily to wait upon
God for it in the use [of] the means of his appointment."
Having first insisted that the means must be used if persons
are to be converted, he then discusses these means under two
headings: duties of natural and of revealed religion. The
three duties of revealed religion here mentioned are: observing the Sabbath, listening to preaching, and using the sacraments. " These," he says, speaking of the sacraments, " ought
to be diligently and carefully attended by all that set themselves to seek the grace of God with such preparation as the
Word of God directs to." Here it seems to be the duty of all
seekers, whether Christians or not, to attend on these ordinances.

Likewise, in the revival sermon on Isa. 40:29-31, Edwards
discusses " waiting on the Lord " with respect to the two
classes, Christians and natural men. Addressing himself to
natural men he urges them to " attend on ordinances " — this
is an important way of waiting on God. We suppose that

" ordinances " includes sacraments. Again: " If we would be in the way of God's grace and blessing we must wait upon him in his own way and in the use of his appointed means." (Ex. 20:24.)

In the sermons above (probably preached before 1740) we find no fencing off of the unregenerate from the Table of the Lord such as is declared in the following sermon delivered to a private meeting in December, 1750, after Edwards had been removed from Northampton for taking the position that the Communion service was for professing Christians only. " Those alone who are born of God are admitted to the privileges of the family of God " is the doctrine based on John 1:5. Everything belonging to the constitution of the visible church represents it as God's family, maintained Edwards; and especially is this true of the Lord's Supper. How unreasonable it is, he argues, to admit to the Lord's Table those who not only do not pretend to be of his family but are admittedly his enemies. Are you, he concludes, admitted to a family in order to be born into it? or are you born into a family and thereby admitted to it? Clearly one must be born of God to be admitted to the family of God and its privileges such as the Communion service. In the application, Edwards urges his hearers to seek regeneration, as he always had done, but absent is an exhortation to use the sacramental means of grace in so seeking, as he had formerly taught.

We do not propose here to go further into this crucial doctrine on which the great controversy that led to Edwards' expulsion from Northampton turned. If the reader wishes to study Edwards' argument, he should read the two fundamental works: *Inquiry Concerning Qualifications for Communion* (*Works,* Vol. I, pp. 281 ff.) and *Misrepresentations Corrected and Truth Vindicated, in Reply to the Rev. Solomon Williams* (*ibid.,* pp. 452 ff.) . Suffice it to notice now that Edwards' evangelistic preaching seems to indicate that he, not only tacitly, but in his pulpit message, at first agreed with the doctrine of Solomon Stoddard which he later repudiated decisively in a controversy that was not only momentous for him personally but for the membership of all New England churches.

CHAPTER XIII

A CALVINISTIC INTERPRETATION
OF BACKSLIDING

"BACKSLIDING" in modern times is usually associated with the Arminian theology, which maintains the possibility of a converted person's falling from grace. In that frame of reference it signifies a converted person's losing his conversion and salvation as a result of sin (Roman Catholic Arminians call such sins " mortal "). Since Calvinism teaches the perseverance of the saints (that is, that converted persons never lose their salvation), it does not accept the doctrine of backsliding in the Arminian sense of the word. The term itself, however, has its place in Calvinistic theology and constantly appears in the preaching of Jonathan Edwards. While I do not recall having ever seen a formal definition of backsliding in his writings, the meaning is quite clear: it is a person's retarding, or desisting from, his seeking of salvation (and not his loss of an already obtained salvation).

In one sermon Edwards lists six different kinds of backsliding (Ps. 78:57). The subject is the backsliding of such as are the visible people of God, that is, those who outwardly profess Christ and thereby become associated with his church. The first, and most grievous, form of backsliding is the commission of the unpardonable sin. Heb., ch. 6 and Mark 3:28 are cited as illustrations of such backsliding. " Backsliding in its perfection is the unpardonable sin. So all backsliding is an (?) approach to it." Second, some apostasize from all religion and become atheists, deists, or profane persons. Third, still others fall into heresy or false religion while not dissociating themselves from the church. A fourth class of backsliders includes those who fall into vicious practices. Fifth, sinners who have been awakened but who have dropped back into their spiritual sleep and death are backsliders — Lot's wife and the children of Israel in the wilderness are Biblical examples of this group, cf. Ps. 78:36 f. And, lastly, there is the falling away of those who have had great affections and shows of godliness, Ps. 106:12. These are the stony-ground hearers of Matt., ch. 13, who receive the Word of God with joy but who recant as soon as tribulations come. Jude, ch. 4, mentions some others of this group, but the Pharisees, as a class, are the best illustration. Saul is a personal illustration. These people either lose their appearance of religion or corrupt their experiences.

Edwards was constantly warning his people against the grave seriousness of the sin of backsliding. It has already been noted that it sometimes led to the unpardonable sin. It was dangerous too, because the backslider was usually incorrigible. It was much more difficult to convert him than others. " And experience confirms that none ordinarily have so much difficulty as backsliders." (Luke 17:32.) Edwards regarded this sin as the one to which Christ referred when he spoke of the man who had one devil driven out, had cleansed his heart and swept and garnished it, and then seven other devils came in and took control and his last condition was worse than the first (Prov. 14:14) .

Backsliding is a treacherous condition. The person who was guilty of this sin hardly realized it; indeed he might think himself well off when he actually was hopelessly doomed. It was compared to the distemper. " It is exceeding secret in its way of working. 'Tis a flattering distemper; it works like a consumption, wherein persons often times flatter themselves that they ben't worse, but hope something better, and in a hopeful way to recover, till a few days before they die." (Luke 17:32.) All in all, this condition was worse than being in hell because there was so little hope of being delivered from it, and while in it one only made his eternal hell the hotter every moment. It would be better if he went to hell than continued in his backslidden condition.

No small amount of attention was given to studying the way that backsliding came about so that Edwards might warn his people what to watch. In the sermon on Job 27:10 the reasons are given for a backsliding in the life of prayer. The doctrine was: " However hypocrites may continue for a season in the duty of prayer, yet it is their manner, after a while, in a great measure to leave it off " (1808, *Works,* Vol. IV, p. 74) . First, hypocrites never have the true spirit of prayer; they never pray for prayer's sake or the glory of God, but for some ulterior purpose. Second, their false hopes, which they entertain thinking themselves to be converted persons, take off the force of God's commands. As long as they feel themselves in danger, they feel constrained to pray; but when they no longer feel such danger they desist from this unpleasant and now unnecessary (as they think) exercise. Third, they now, feeling safe, dare to neglect the duty of prayer. A fourth reason that they backslide from their life of prayer is that they had never, at the outset, counted the cost of the Christian life. They had wrongly supposed that it would be an easy life, that it would require very little effort. When they discover other-wise, they are offended and disillusioned and tend to give up in despair and to revert to sinful practices. This is not con-genial to a life of prayer, for " sinning and praying don't very well agree together." Finally, because they have no interest in the gracious spiritual promises of God to keep their prayers alive, they tend to lapse.

The sermon on Prov. 26:11 gives a more fundamental explanation of the spiritual phenomenon of backsliding. The doctrine of the sermon is: " Wicked men though for a while they may seem to forsake their sins yet if their natures are not changed they will be very liable to return to them again." Three reasons for this are here given. First, " Nature is a more powerful principle of action than anything that opposes it." It cannot be conquered by anything external to it. If it is not changed, it cannot be quenched. Second, nature is more constant than anything else in the affairs of men. Convictions come and go; awakenings are now and then; resolutions are made and broken; but, a man's nature remains the same and constant in its activity. Third, God gives no promise of continual assistance against the nature of a man. While he works against it by the convictions of conscience and the activity of the Spirit, he does not promise to continue always to strive with men. So, if the nature remains unchanged and the activity of God is changed, when men do not repent and believe, there is nothing to resist the activity of this nature and it prevails. A voice from heaven could not stop Israel in the wilderness; the terrors of hell cannot overcome this nature; promises and resolutions are of no adequate avail.

Perhaps the best illustration of a backslider to whom Edwards devoted much attention is King Saul. The sermon on I Sam. 28:15 (preached in February, 1732–1733) is an extensive study of Saul's experiences: " Saul was a remarkable instance of the awful and doleful circumstances a man is in when left of God." First of all, Edwards notes that there was a time when God was with Saul. God was not with him as he was with the saints, but he outwardly blessed him. He hon-

ored him in the sight of Israel, and appointed him king by
an immediate revelation of the divine will. Therefore he was
called the Lord's anointed, I Sam. 24:6. Because God thus
honored the king, his prophet Samuel did the same. When
the king consulted him, Samuel inquired of God on his be-
half and this was a further evidence that God was with him.
Providence, generally, was with him and he was victorious in
battle.

In addition to these outward blessings of God, Saul enjoyed
considerable measure of the gifts of the Holy Spirit. He had
zeal for the cause of Jehovah, as was seen in his destroying
those who had familiar spirits as God had commanded. He
kept sin from his army. And in spite of his great prominence,
he was humble appearing and he held his peace against the
children of Belial, I Sam. 10:17. Saul had extraordinary gifts
and assurances of God's Spirit. The spirit of prophecy was
given to him. His ability was by the Holy Spirit, I Sam. 10:6,
and the Holy Spirit was on him, I Sam. 13:14.

In spite of all these advantages, however, Saul was not turn-
ing to God and God was gradually abandoning him. But the
crisis came when, contrary to the express divine command,
Saul spared King Agag. Then the kingdom was taken from
him, I Sam. 13:14.

From that time on there was nothing from God but a curse.
Saul had backslidden and God had permanently abandoned
him. Henceforth the king had no more quietness of mind. He
suffered torments of the damned. Before these acute inner
sufferings he tended to give up rather than to strive more earnestly than ever. Corresponding to his inner turmoil, his outward affairs failed to prosper. Jealousy of David, distrust of
Jonathan, and defeats by the Philistines marred his reign.
Then the restraining grace of God was removed and Saul, being abandoned by God, abandoned himself and a murderous

mood overtook him as he killed eighty-five priests of Jehovah, broke his oath, and finally killed himself.

Jonathan Edwards did not see backsliding in King Saul, Judas, and Israel alone; it was marring the great work of God in Northampton also. In spite of all his warnings against this fatal spiritual malady, many of his people fell the victims of it. In 1744, after the revivals were a memory, a letter of his gives a general appraisal of the past, acknowledging the backsliding of many and hopeful of the perseverance of most:

" 'Tis probable that you have been informed, by other correspondents, before now, what the present state of things in New England is: it is indeed, on many accounts, very melancholy: there is a vast alteration within these two years; for about so long I think it is, since the Spirit of God began to withdraw, and this great work has been on the decline. Great numbers in the land, about two years ago, were raised to an exceedingly great height, in joy and elevation of mind; and through want of watchfulness, and sensibleness of the danger and temptation that there is in such circumstances, many were greatly exposed, and the devil taking the advantage, multitudes were soon, and to themselves insensibly, led far away from God and their duty; God was provoked that he was not sanctified in this height of advancement, as he ought to have been, he saw our spiritual pride and self-confidence, and the polluted flames that arose of intemperate, unhallowed zeal; and he soon, in a great measure, withdrew from us; and the consequence has been, that the Enemy has come in like a flood, in various respects, until the deluge has overwhelmed the whole land. There had, from the beginning, been a great mixture, especially in some places, of false experiences, and false Religion with true; but from about this time, the mixture became much greater, many were led away with sad delusions; and this opened the door for the Enemy to come in like a flood in another respect, it gave great advantages to these enemies and opposers of this work, furnished them with weapons and gave them new courage, and has laid the friends of the work under such disadvantage, that nothing that they could do would avail any thing to withstand their violence. And now it is come to that, that the work is put to stop every where, and it is a day of the Enemy's triumph: but I believe also a day of God's People's Humiliation, which will be better to them in the end than their elevations and raptures. The time has been amongst us when the sower went forth to sow, and we have seen the spring, wherein the seed sprang up in different sorts of ground, appearing then fair and flourishing; but this spring is past, and we now see the summer, wherein the sun is up with a burning heat, that tries the sorts of ground; and now appears the difference, the seed in stony ground, where there was only a thin layer of earth on a rock, withers away, the moisture being dried out; and the hidden seeds and roots of thorns, in unsubdued ground, now springs up and chokes the seed of the word. Many high professors are fallen, some into gross immoralities, some into a rooted spiritual pride, enthusiasm, and an incorrigible wildness of behaviour, some into a cold frame of mind, showing a great indifference to the things of Religion. But there are many, and I hope those the greater part of those that were professed Converts, who appear hitherto like the good ground, and notwithstanding the thick and dark clouds, that so soon follow that blessed sunshine that we have had; yet I cannot but stedfastly maintain a hope and persuasion that God will revive his work, and that what has been so great and very extraordinary, is a forerunner of a yet more glorious and extensive work . . ." (Dwight *Works*, Vol. I, pp. 212–213) .

CHAPTER XIV

THE LIGHT SHINES IN THE DARKNESS

ALL THE STEPS that we have thus far examined have been steps that may have been in vain. In other words, awakened persons may have, after their convictions, been hardened or undecided or not thorough. On the other hand, they may have been sufficiently awakened to begin a true seeking for their salvation, driven on by the unworthy but useful motive of self-interest. They may have cultivated the special days of opportunity when God was near to bless and save. Nevertheless, they may still have backslidden or for some other reason never found that for which they sought. So all their endeavors may have come to nothing so far as their actual salvation is concerned, although even futile seeking would have had the utility of preventing greater sins and greater damnation.

While all of these steps may have been of no avail to the salvation of the soul, they were indispensable to it. These steps must normally have been taken before any person was given the grace of conversion. God, though sovereign, was disposed to give his great mercy to those who were in a way of seeking. It is that gift to which we now come, the goal toward which all the striving has tended. The light shines in the darkness.

The point at which God actually engages the human soul

117

savingly is the point of knowledge. We have already observed that nothing can happen to anyone of a religious nature without knowledge. Unless people hear the gospel and receive the outward call, they will never have convictions, impressions, awakenings, seekings, or anything. And as we have seen, this knowledge must be sound Biblical knowledge. Unregenerate persons may have this knowledge — " may yet have an intellectual opinion about divine things, as a man may have some knowledge or opinion about sweet things who has not tasted them." This is strictly an external or merely speculative knowledge which they have. God communicates himself differently to them than he does to regenerate persons: " The Spirit of God acts in a very different manner in the one case, from what he doth in the other. He may indeed act *upon* the mind of a natural man; but he acts *in* the mind of a saint as an *indwelling vital principle.* He acts upon the mind of an unregenerate person as an *extrinsick occasional agent;* for in acting upon them, he doth not unite himself to them . . ." (*The Divine and Supernatural Light,* Boston, 1734, p. 7).

Even the devil may have this speculative knowledge. Furthermore, he does have it. " The devil is orthodox in his faith; he believes the true scheme of doctrine; he is no *Deist, Socinian, Arian, Pelagian,* or *Antimonian;* the articles of his faith are all sound, and what he is thoroughly established in." (*True Grace Distinguished from the Experience of Devils,* New York, 1753, pp. 13–14.) In such a sermon it was not difficult for Edwards to convince the New Light Presbyterian Synod that although it was uncommon for unregenerate *men* to be orthodox, it was possible.

Such speculative knowledge, which was possible for unregenerate men and devils, was therefore not sufficient for salvation. " Nothing in the mind of man, that is of the same nature with what the devils experience, or are the subjects of, is any sure sign of saving grace." (*Ibid.*, p. 4.)

Thus, according to Edwards, men could have sound knowledge without being regenerated, but they could not be regenerated without having sound knowledge. Thorough conviction of the understanding is the root and foundation of all religion (Matt. 13:23, doctrine 2). Faith is a rational act and no man ever yet exercised true faith but that he see reason that he should do so (II Cor. 13:5). " It is not according to the nature of the human soul, to love an object which is entirely unknown. . . . Such is the nature of man, that nothing can come at the heart, but through the door of the understanding: And there can be no spiritual knowledge of that of which there is not first a rational knowledge." (*Works,* Vol. VIII, p. 10.)

What, then, is the function of the Spirit in illuminating the minds of men savingly? He " helps us to receive the revelation in the Word." Men hear of the loveliness of Christ, but until they receive illumination, " they have no taste to relish that sweetness any more than an image of stone could taste honey if you should put it into its mouth " (Matt. 13:5). The Spirit does not, Edwards, quoting " Mr. Stoddard," says, " reveal new truths not revealed in the Word." The Spirit's communication is not a " secret whisper," that is, not the imparting of new propositions (Luke 14:26).

The nature of the interworking of the divine and supernatural light with natural reason is made clear in this sermon on Matt. 16:17: " 'Tis by reason, that we become possessed of a notion of those doctrines that are the subject matter of this *divine light;* and reason may many ways be indirectly, and remotely an advantage to it. And reason has also to do in the acts that are immediately consequent on this discovery: A seeing the truth of religion from hence, is by reason; though it be but by one step, and the inference be immediate. So reason has to do in that accepting of, and trusting in *Christ,* that is consequent on it. But, if we take reason strictly, not for the faculty of mental perception in general, but for ratiocination, or a power of inferring by arguments; I say if we take reason thus, the perceiving of spiritual beauty and excellency no more belongs to reason, than it belongs to the sense of feeling to perceive colours, or to the power of seeing to perceive the sweetness of food. It is out of reason's province to perceive the beauty or loveliness of any thing: Such a perception don't belong to that faculty. Reason's work is to perceive truth, and not excellency. 'Tis not ratiocination that gives men the perception of the beauty and amiableness of a countenance . . . It depends on the sense of the heart. Reason may determine that a countenance is beautiful to others, it may determine that honey is sweet to others; but it will never give me a perception of its sweetness" (*The Divine and Supernatural Light,* Boston, 1734, pp. 27-28).

In other words, the divine and supernatural light is only light — it is not itself knowledge. Religious knowledge comes by the reason, the natural reason, but the " beauty " or " excellency " or " amiableness " of this knowledge is not seen by natural reason until the divine and supernatural light reveals it — to the natural reason. This divine light comes from God and its experience in the regenerate is called " the sense of the heart " in distinction from the ratiocination of the mind. Though distinct from the discursive intelligence, it is not, however, separable from it. Only when there is previous doctrinal knowledge in the mind, by means of natural reason, can the " sense of the heart " reveal its beauty. Edwards would say: religious concepts without the sense of the heart are empty; the sense of the heart without the religious conceptions is blind. Edwards' theory of religious knowledge may be represented by the photographic developing process. When the picture is first taken on the emulsion nothing appears or can be seen. When the film is developed the picture is seen. The developer adds nothing to the picture that is not already present, but it makes the picture visible. Natural men may have a religious picture on their mind, they may have many such pictures, they may have many more than regenerate persons and, indeed, much better pictures, but not a one of these fine pictures is ever developed. The divine and supernatural light is the developer God uses to make the beauty and sweetness of divine truth apparent to the regenerate.

This analogy, incidentally, shows the epistemological difference between Edwards and Kant. In Kant's theory, the developing process adds essential ingredients to the original picture which is hopelessly confused without it. The " categories " are actually imposed in the process. In Edwards' theory, the developing does not add a single ingredient to the original picture that comes to the mind. The picture is complete when taken. The developing merely — but this is the all-important step, of course — makes the picture visible.

The great incentive to the natural man to study the Bible, though he does not see its beauty, is evident. The more he knows in his unconverted state the more will he apprehend if God ever converts him. " The more you have of a rational knowledge of the things of the gospel the more opportunity will there be, when the Spirit shall be breathed into your heart, to see the excellency of these things, and to taste the sweetness of them." There is the further consideration, also, that even God cannot make the beauty of ideas appear when such are not present. God cannot make something appear beautiful when that something does not exist at all.

The " divine and supernatural light " is the theme of many sermons. " 'Tis a sight of the glory of God in Christ is that and that only which changes the elect of God and makes 'em like God." (II Cor. 3:18; Andover.) " There never was any man," Edwards says in another sermon, " that once came to understand what manner of one Christ was but his heart was infallibly drawn to him." (John 6:45.) In still another sermon he affirms that true love and knowledge of God assimilates to God and makes men a partaker of his nature (Matt. 15:26). In I Cor. 2:14 (Andover), he shows that the opposite also is true. " There is a spiritual understanding of divine things, which all natural and unregenerate men are destitute of." In II Cor. 2:19, he maintained that this spiritual knowledge was above all that the wicked could have.

It is because of the nature of this spiritual knowledge that Edwards can say, " There is none that teaches like God " (Job 36:22). There are four ways mentioned in which human teachers are inferior to God: None can impart the will to do what is taught; none can impart a knowledge so excellent; none can teach so effectually; and none can make the disciple love what he hated.

In spite of the close relation between the divine light and doctrinal knowledge, this light was not primarily intellectual, but affectional. While the intellectual was the necessary foundation of this vision the vision was more than the intellectual. What exactly it was Edwards makes abundantly clear. It was a sight of the " amiableness " of the divine attributes (II Cor. 3:18; Andover). The attributes could be understood apart from the divine light, but their amiableness could not otherwise be seen. Devils could have a knowledge of the attributes but not of their beauty. The godly only have a " sensible " apprehension of the main things of the gospel (Matt. 13:23).

Preaching on II Cor. 2:19, Edwards discusses this saving experience not in terms of light but of smell. " The spiritual knowledge of Christ is as it were a sweet savor that the soul hath of Christ." Five points of resemblance to the olfactory

experience are noted. First, in smelling it is the good and excellent nature of the object that is perceived. Second, in
smelling we have an immediate perception of the good.
Third, " in smelling or tasting, a sweet savor a knowledge or
idea is obtained of the excellency of a thing perfectly diverse
in its nature and kind from all that can be obtained any other
way." Four, if we have a savor, the good perceived is perceived as excellent. Five, necessarily this experience implies
approbation and therein differs from speculation.

Not only is the divine light more than speculative knowledge, but it seems to be necessary for fully correct speculative
knowledge. This point is not much developed in Edwards,
and many of his remarks, such as those concerning the excellent speculative knowledge of the devils, seem opposed to
it. However, the sermon on Matt. 13:23 speaks of the new
judgments of the godly as they see in the Word the " intrinsic
signatures of divinity." " There are signatures of divine majesty to be seen in the word, and signatures of divine wisdom
and of divine holiness, and the evident marks of divine grace
that make it evident that the word of God did proceed from a
divine majesty, and wisdom and holiness and grace. There are
as proper manifestations of divinity in the speech of God as
there are manifestations of humanity in the speech of men.
God opens the understandings of profitable hearers to see
these signatures and manifestations of divinity, so that they
hear it as the word of God. They do as it were hear God
speak."

Illumination is dependent on knowledge. Knowledge is not
dependent in the same sense, on illumination, but illumination does powerfully promote knowledge. Once God has
made the knowledge come alive, the saints develop an eager
desire for more of such knowledge that more experience may
be possible. Thus the sense of the heart promotes the interests

of the head. " It will also be allowed, that the spiritual saving knowledge of God, and divine things, greatly promotes speculative knowledge; as it engages the mind in its search into things of this kind, and much assists to a distinct understanding of them; so that, other things being equal, they that have spiritual knowledge, are much more likely than others, to have a good doctrinal acquaintance with things of religion; but yet, such acquaintance may be no distinguishing characteristic of true saints." (*True Grace Distinguished from the Experience of Devils*, New York, 1753, p. 13.)

The sermon on Heb. 5:12, the doctrine of which is: " Every Christian should make a business of endeavoring to grow in knowledge in divinity " (*Works*, Vol. VIII, p. 6) , is especially devoted to this point. " It doubtless," he preached to his congregation, " concerns every one to endeavor to excel in the knowledge of things which pertain to his profession or principal calling. If it concerns men to excel in anything, or in any wisdom or knowledge at all, it certainly concerns them to excel in the affairs of their main profession and work. But the calling and work of every Christian is to live to God. This is said to be his *high calling*, Phil. iii.14. This is the business, and if I may so speak, the *trade* of a Christian, his main work, and indeed should be his only work. No business should be done by a Christian, but as it is some way or other a part of this. Therefore certainly the Christian should endeavor to be well acquainted with those things which belong to this work." (*ibid.*, pp. 19–20) .

While there is a divine illumination that marks the moment of conversion, these visions are given intermittently throughout the life of the Christian. They are usually brief disclosures of glory comparable to the sun coming from behind clouds. The beloved is like a roe on the mountains (II Cor. 13:5) . But this glimpse is reassuring. It is not the length of time, but the nature of the view, that guarantees the presence of the beloved. A contemporary Scottish minister, Ebenezer Erskine, spoke much of " blinks " by which he apparently referred to these enriching, but infrequent, views of the divine glory. As Erskine became older he relied less on them, an indication, perhaps, of the truth of Edwards' statement that they are infrequently given. The purpose of these views, discoveries, or blinks is not that beholders should stay on the mount of transfiguration or stand gazing into heaven, but radiate the light to others. Thus Edwards appeals to " those that have lately been enlightened — don't only be enlightened but shine " (Cant. 6:10).

BORN FROM ABOVE

No NATURAL MAN, says Edwards, makes choice of God until he is converted (Ruth 1:16). Divine illumination
alone does not account, therefore, for a person's becoming a
Christian. There must be a nature that loves the divine and
supernatural light. " Except a man be born again he cannot
see the kingdom of God." These words of Christ's are taken
as the doctrine of a sermon on John 3:3 dealing with the nature of regeneration. The early sermon on Prov. 27:22 has
this doctrine: " Folly is naturally so rooted and confirmed in
men that if God leaves them to themselves let what will be
done with them they will not learn wisdom."

" 'Tis no wonder that Christ said that we must be born
again." (John 3:7.) In this sermon Edwards surveys the en-
tire Bible to show that everywhere it teaches the necessity of
the new birth. Then he proceeds to show what is meant by
regeneration. For one thing, it means the changing of all that
we received by the first birth (morally speaking) ; and, for
another, that this change must be universal, not dealing with
aspects of a person merely, but with the total person.

Furthermore, the new birth is not something external, but
internal; nor is it merely internal, but supernatural as well.
If it were merely an internal change in the resolutions and

habits, Nicodemus would not have been so surprised. He would have seen nothing mysterious in this. Moreover, it is a radical change and not some superficial mending of the character. The person dies to law, to sin, and to the world, becoming not only a new creature but a new creation also. Finally, this new birth is not a work of the newborn person any more than his first birth was.

That there must be such a change as conversion, Edwards deduces from three arguments. First, it is impossible for a man with a filthy, sinful heart to cleanse his heart by means of a filthy heart. If his depravity were partial, as the Arminians suppose, this would be possible; but since man is utterly dead in sin, it is not possible. Second, if it were not necessary that a man be born from above, the infinity of Christ's atonement would have been out of all proportion to what was necessary. God would have done, in the giving of his Son, infinitely more than was necessary. This would be an impossible reflection on his intelligence. And, in the third place, there would be no proportion between the real and the relative relationship of a saint if the new birth were not a supernatural necessity. That is to say, since men by conversion are brought into the most intimate, filial relation to God, there must be something proportionate on which such a relationship rests. If men were actually children of God without having the divine nature, there would be no meaning to the relation. So, since the elect are brought into the family of God, it must be because they have the new nature from God; that is, it must be because they have been born again from above, from the Spirit of God.

The argument presented above was that the Bible taught that there was such a thing as conversion and that, if there was such, it must have been supernatural in character. But in a sermon on a text a few verses later in this same discourse

with Nicodemus, Edwards argues the fact of conversion.
" There is such a thing as conversion." (John 3:10-11.) Only
one of his arguments here is that the Bible teaches it; the
other seven are drawn from reason. First, man is manifestly
made to be happy; but equally obviously his happiness must
be in union with God. Animals, Edwards remarks, may be
happy with this world, but man was made for higher things
and cannot rest until he finds his rest in God. Union with God
can only be effected by God himself. Man cannot unite himself to God; only God can unite himself to man. Therefore,
the argument runs, if there is to be happiness for man, there
must be a birth from above. Reason also teaches, secondly,
that union with God is impossible without holiness, Amos
3:3. Only God can make man holy enough for his fellowship.
Third, and this is the theme of much of his later work on
Original Sin, reason shows that men are universally corrupt
and in bondage. They cannot convert themselves. This is
made even more explicit in argument four: nature cannot be
changed by nature. A nature cannot influence the nature to be
different than its nature. So if man is to be happy and blessed,
he must be changed supernaturally, reason demands. We will
mention only one other argument that is given in this sermon: namely, the practical one drawn from the changed lives
of many persons. There have been thousands who have been
made other than they were, and they could not have done it
themselves. He cites especially the notoriously wicked who
were converted to show from what depths men have been
changed, and the martyrs to show to what heights men have
been lifted. There is nothing like the quantity or quality of
martyrs in any other religion. He concludes: " Reason teaches
it so much that unless we deny the being of God we can't
avoid acknowledging such a thing as conversion." The doctrine is applied in a seventeen-point application.

Regeneration consists in the divine infusion of a new nature. It is a gracious principle in the soul (*Works,* Vol. IV, p. 130). This is no mere alteration of habits or outward behavior, but a change on the inside. It is " physical " (in the realistic sense of the word) and not merely moral. The nature of man consists of principles of perception and principles of action. Human nature differs from animal nature in the possession of principles. Some of these distinctly human principles are the faculties, the natural appetites, the love of honor, the love of pleasure, and the aversion to pain. Elsewhere, Edwards says the new principles are not new faculties and defines " principles " as " that foundation which is laid in nature, . . . for any particular manner or kind of exercise of the faculties of the soul; or a natural habit or foundation for action " (*Works,* Vol. IV, p. 135). " But man when he is changed from a sinner to a saint has new principles of perception and action; principles that are entirely diverse and not arising merely from [a] new disposition of the old or contracted habits as those changes that are wrought by education do. They are principles that are vastly superior to those he had before." (John 3:3.) They are not derived from these native principles. It is no more possible, Edwards insists, for them to come from these than for rational creatures to come from brutes without physical change. There is a divine infusion of spiritual principles of understanding and action above anything before possessed.

Furthermore, this is a change of the whole man, a universal change. The total change takes place immediately. Just as a child, when newly born, possesses all its parts of body and soul, so it is with the spiritual child (Eph. 4:24; I Thess. 5:23). Even his body is in a sense new. This point Edwards develops more fully in a sermon on I Thess. 5:23. " In true conversion men's bodies are in some respect changed as well as their souls."

A third characteristic of regeneration is that the person receives being, very much as at his first conception. At the fall he virtually lost everything (Edwards makes clear, elsewhere, that he lost everything of the moral image of God). Therefore, in regeneration, he is newly created, Eph. 2:5. In the fourth place, newly born, he finds himself in a new world, as well. Fifth, at the same time that he is a new creation in a new world, he is such by the use of means. As the first birth takes place by the instrumentality of human parents, human means are also used in conversion. The last two characteristics are closely related to each other as well as to the preceding. The regenerate are like children: imperfect, immature, incomplete, but growing. At the same time, being children they are members of a family, in this case, the family of God.

Other sermons and writings develop this theme, though not so fully. Commenting on Matt. 7:15, Edwards asks what is the essential difference between true Christians and merely nominal ones. He finds it to be the difference between the substance and life of Christianity versus the mere shadow. It is the difference between a real man and a picture. " A work of conversion is a great effect of God's power and grace in the heart. [It] is not a mere whim or fancy but a great and certain reality." (I Cor. 6:11.)

This principle of holiness in the soul seems to be none other than the Holy Spirit himself. This is taught in the first published sermon: *God Glorified in the Work of Redemption, by the Greatness of Man's Dependence Upon Him, in the Whole of it,* Boston, 1731. It is more developed in a 1746 sermon on Gal. 3:13-14. " The Holy Spirit or the third person of the Trinity in his operations and fruits is the sum of the blessings that Christ purchased for us in the work of our redemption." Edwards gives no less than twelve arguments to prove this doctrine. In the latter part of the sermon, he explains how these fruits are from the Holy Spirit. Specifically, he insists that they are not merely by the Spirit but consist in the Spirit. The Holy Spirit is the principle of life and happiness of all the saints. All spiritual life consists in divine love; but this is nothing other than the Holy Spirit, I Peter 5:13; I John 3:24; 4:12-13. Christ is the olive tree and the Spirit is the very sap, Zech., ch. 7. The Spirit is to the soul as breath is to the body. He is the fullness of the creature's life and glory. And in this manner Edwards construes the words of Peter, "partakers of the divine nature." This explains also Edwards' observation that Christ gives good works to believers rather than they giving them to him (Phil. 4:19). We are his workmanship in Christ Jesus. We do good works as we have the Spirit and we have the Spirit only as, and in the measure that, Christ gives him to us. Edwards sees the essence of what Christ has purchased for believers in the covenant of grace to be the Holy Spirit (cf. also the sermon on Phil. 1:21).

In the *Divine and Supernatural Light* sermon, this principle is said to "exist in the soul habitually, and according to such a stated constitution or law, that lays such a foundation for exercises in a continued course, as is called a *principle* of nature. Not only are remaining *principles* assisted to do their work more freely and fully, but those principles are restored that were utterly destroyed by the fall; and the mind thenceforward habitually exerts those acts that the dominion of sin had made it as wholly destitute of, as a dead body is of vital acts." In I John 3:9, the doctrine is "that grace is in the hearts of the saints in this world as a seed," while in the sermon on II Peter 1:19 this life is compared to the rising of the daystar. It is a spark, according to the sermon on John 1:16.

In other sermons, there are some indications that this new life is nothing less than the life of God. Even apart from the sermons on Galatians, which give more attention to this doctrine than other sermons do, we find hints in John 3:10-11 where Edwards identifies conversion with union with God. In the same gospel, ch. 14:23, in a sermon preached in 1733, the doctrine developed is: "They that love Christ and obey Christ God and Christ will come to them and dwell with them." In The First Epistle of John 3:1, it is noted that the saint's life is Christ and therefore is eternal life, while in a sermon on Eph. 2:5-7 we find it said that "there is more of God in it" (conversion) "than in almost any other work."

The clearest and fullest statement that the Spirit is the foundation of regeneration is found in the *Treatise on Grace,* which was not published until 1865. "I suppose there is no other principle of grace in the soul than the very Holy Ghost dwelling in the soul and acting there as a vital principle. To speak of a habit of grace as a natural disposition to act grace, as begotten in the soul by the first communication of Divine light, and as the natural and necessary consequence of the first light, it seems in some respects to carry a wrong idea with it. Indeed the first exercise of grace in the first light has a tendency to future acts, as from an abiding principle, by grace and by the covenant of God; but not by any natural force. The giving one gracious discovery or act of grace, or a thousand, has no proper natural tendency to cause an abiding habit of grace for the future; nor any otherwise than by Divine constitution and covenant. But all succeeding acts of grace must be as immediately, and, to all intents and purposes, as much from the immediate acting of the Spirit of God on the soul, as the first; and if God should take away His Spirit out of the soul, all habits and acts of grace would of themselves cease as immediately as light ceases in a room when a candle is carried out. And no man has a habit of grace dwelling in him any otherwise than as he has the Holy Spirit dwelling in him in his temple, and acting in union with his natural faculties, after the manner of a vital principle. So that when they act grace, 'tis, in the language of the Apostle, ' not they, but Christ living in them.' Indeed the Spirit of God, united to human faculties, acts very much after the manner of a natural principle or habit. So that one act makes way for another, and so it now settles the soul in a disposition to holy acts; but that it does, so as by grace and covenant, and not from any natural necessity." (Alexander B. Grosart, ed., *Selections of Unpublished Works of Jonathan Edwards,* p. 55.) This explains the statement in the sermon on Luke 22:31: " There is no essential difference between that principle of grace which believers have and that original holiness which our first parents and the angels had." Edwards thought of original righteousness as nothing other than the indwelling of the Spirit, and of the Fall as his departure.

The degree to which believers possess the Holy Spirit in this life is but an earnest of the fullness with which they shall later receive him, Eph. 1:14. Edwards often speaks of the meager degree of grace that saints in this life possess. In his *Original Sin,* he estimates that sin has far more expression in the Christian than virtue (though it is not the prevailing principle) . " What considerate person is there, even among the more virtuous part of mankind, but would be ashamed to say, and profess before God or men, that he loves God half so much as he ought to do; or that he exercises one half of that esteem, honor, and gratitude towards God, which would be altogether becoming him; considering what God is, and what great manifestations he has made of his transcendent excellency and goodness, and what benefits he receives from him? And if few or none of the best of men can with reason and truth make even such a profession, how far from it must the generality of mankind be? " (*Works,* Vol. VI, p. 167.) At the end of this section Edwards is obliged to consider an objection: " That the argument seems to prove too much, in that it will prove, that even good men themselves have more sin than holiness; which also has been supposed. But if this were true, it would follow, that sin is the prevalent principle even in good men, and that it is the principle which has the predominancy in the heart and practice of the truly pious; which is plainly contrary to the word of God.

" I answer, if it be indeed so, that there is more sin, consisting in defect of required holiness, than there is of holiness in good men in this world; yet it will not follow that sin has the chief government of their heart and practice, for two reasons . . ." (*Ibid.*, p. 172.)

A particularly interesting discourse is the revival sermon on John 6:45 which explains in psychological terms how regeneration actually works. The doctrine states the matter generally and the development breaks the doctrine down into its parts. " There never was any man that once came to understand what manner of one Christ was but his heart was infallibly drawn to him."

Edwards begins his development empirically, considering the actual phenomena of conversion. When men once do see Christ, all their corruptions cannot keep them from him. It is a simple and often observed fact that the moment the sinner really sees the loveliness of Christ he cannot be held back by the sins that previously kept him in bondage. Nor can any of the supposed arguments that he had against Christianity, and which often caused him to stumble previously and remain hesitating in unbelief, restrain him once he has seen Christ. Even Satan, his cruel master who could drive him to gather sticks for his own funeral pyre, cannot hold him now. The strong man is bound when once the believer sees Jesus and hears him calling; the devil is now impotent; his prey is snatched from his teeth. And not only certain men, but all types of men, react in the same way when once they have understood what manner of man Christ is. They are irresistibly drawn to him.

But why does it work this way? Edwards now asks. For two reasons: because of the nature of the discoverer (Edwards means revealer), and because of the nature of what is discovered (revealed). In this experience God himself is exerting himself. He comes into the soul on rays of illuminating light. So, there is omnipotence in the soul (citing II Tim. 3:5). Furthermore, what is revealed is, in its very nature, as appealing as the God who exerts himself in the revelation. Christ is seen in all his excellency, and this powerfully draws the entranced soul that beholds him. Also Christ's wonderful grace and love are the center of this revelation, and when one sees such glory how can he be unmoved? He cannot; he must come, drawn by his own affections. And if he feels any reluctance, because of the consciousness of his own sin and unworthiness, the vision of the sufficiency of Christ's pardon and his faithfulness to forgive all who come in repentance overcomes that momentary reluctance, and the sinner comes running. Thus Christ infallibly draws the soul that beholds him, and thus Edwards explains the meaning of the doctrine of irresistible grace.

It may seem strange in the light of what has just been said to find this statement in another sermon: " When men under convictions are put upon fleeing, it is a mere force, 'tis because God lays hold on their hands, as he did on Lot's, and his wife's, and drags them out " (Luke 17:32). But this is another aspect of the experience. Here God is not changing the nature, but overcoming it. In the case of Lot's wife, who never was converted, that is all that God did do. Lot, who was a converted man and therefore a man whose nature had been changed, did not have the corruptions of his old nature removed and hence God was obliged, on occasions such as this, to overcome that nature (as he did before he was converted). But the saving acceptance of Christ is not forced, but voluntary. None, Edwards insists, is forced to come to Christ (Gen. 24:58) ; it is a " free choice." They shall be made willing in the day of God's power. And so he pleads for a free response to his invitation: " God has sent me to you to make you the offer. Christ has sent me to give you an invitation."

So, then, the invitation is given to all, and no one who gets Christ gets him any other way than by a " free choice." Nevertheless, no natural man, says Edwards, makes choice of God until that man is converted (Ruth 1:16). God must first choose us before we choose him. Our choice rests on his sovereignty. It is but a peradventure, whether God will ever give them repentance to the acknowledging of the truth (Acts 16:29). When God does give this grace, no man will resist because no man can resist the loveliness of Christ when once he sees it. Edwards scores the Arminian doctrine of resistance to grace (Rom. 8:29).

We may conclude this section with a question concerning the relation between regeneration and illumination. Both mark the very beginning of the Christian life. How are they related to each other? They seem in their beginning not to be mutually dependent. That is, the illumination does not seem to depend on the regeneration, nor the regeneration on the illumination. The illumination comes from God immediately, not from the nature, even the regenerate nature, of man. Nor can the regeneration come from the illumination. The amiableness of the divine attributes is always there, but it is never seen by the carnal nature of man. The natural man is totally destitute of this " knowledge." Therefore, when a person sees the light he is no longer an unconverted person. Unconverted persons cannot see it in order to become changed. They must be changed in order to see it. Therefore the conversion must come directly from God even as the light does. But they must come simultaneously. When the light dawns, at that very moment the spiritual eyes are opened. These two phenomena are not causally related, it would seem, but only occasionally. This is Edwards' soteriological " pre-established harmony."

CHAPTER

XVI

JUSTIFICATION BY FAITH ALONE

IN SPITE of the very elaborate steps to salvation of Edwards and the Puritans, salvation itself was held to be immediately received at the very moment true faith was exercised. Regeneration and illumination having taken place by the sovereign pleasure and power of God, faith is born in the elect soul.

Joseph Tracy, in *The Great Awakening*, makes the simplicity of this very doctrine the secret of Edwards' success as a revivalist. Edwards showed, he said, that " God has not appointed any thing for men to do before coming to Christ by faith . . ." (p. 10). Tracy is not unaware of Edwards' doctrine of seeking but is observing that faith was all that was necessary — anything else was merely in order to receive faith. Edwards opened the door to Christ and he opened it wide. The people came in.

Faith, for Edwards, begins in the understanding. It is a rational act, in the first instance (II Cor. 13:5). We have already observed, in our discussion of the relation of doctrine and illumination, that truth must be present before it can be illumined. The same fact is seen in the matter of faith. There must be that which is to be believed, before it can be believed. There must be an object of faith before there can be an exer-

138

cise of it. Edwards, in a sermon on Hab. 2:4, indicates that the nature of faith is acquiescence of the soul in the divine sufficiency. It is apparent that there must be some notion of what this divine sufficiency is before the soul can acquiesce in it. In the same sermon faith is said to be " that by which the soul is united to Christ." The soul cannot be united to Christ consciously without knowing something about him. Likewise, when Edwards, preaching on Hos. 1:11, says that " they that do truly believe in Christ do therein by their own act appoint Christ to be their head," he implies an understanding of Christ whom they appoint as their head.

It is apparent from what has already been said, that Edwards is not at all satisfied to let the definition of faith rest with the delineation of its rational element. While he is quite insistent that faith must begin in the understanding and cannot exist without knowledge, he is far more concerned to stress other features of faith.

He has already defined faith in terms of acquiescence. This is an assent of the soul to what it understands. This assent is more significant than knowledge, for many may have true knowledge who do not have this necessary acquiescence. In his discussion of faith, in the sermon on Hos. 1:11, he goes into the matter thoroughly, showing that unbelievers do not really want to believe in Christ. Therein they are distinguished from true believers, who gladly acquiesce in their knowledge of Christ. Unbelievers may have the knowledge, but never the acquiescence.

Justifying faith is not only of the understanding. He stresses this truth in the important sermon on Rom. 4:16, the doctrine of which is " that the grace of God in the New Covenant eminently appears in that it proposes justification only by faith." Understanding, inclination, and will are all involved in true faith. Anything less than this is not justifying

faith. " Saving faith differs from all common faith in its nature, kind and essence," he preached in a later sermon on
I John 5:1. " Faith is a uniting with Christ, not a mere recog-
nition of his existence. Love is a distinguishing property of
a saving faith " (Gal. 5:6) . Love, he says there, always attends
and is implied in saving faith. It is the whole soul's receiving
Christ. Indeed, true faith is effectual by means of the divine
love that is implied in it. This is stated still more explicitly
in the same sermon (Gal. 5:6) . " Only that sort of faith that
works by love avails anything before God." The receiving of
Christ must be of the heart, he says, because Christ stands at
the door of the heart. In this sermon he again insists on faith's
being an assent of the soul, an act of the will and inclination,
a venturing one's whole interest on Christ. So, the " saints do
live by faith." (Hab. 2:4.)

It may help us to understand Edwards' doctrine of faith if
we consider his discussion of false, or superficial, faith. In his
exposition of Matt. 13:5, in the series of sermons on the parable of the sower, he observes that belief involves three acts,
each one of which may be spurious in some persons. Thus
there is an intellectual, an emotional, and a volitional element. But these may come about in some persons because of
their training or education and not because of a truly personal assent at all. There are those who seem to believe in the
truth, but it is because of the authority of some minister.
They feel compelled to believe what he says because it is he
who says it. This is not genuine faith in God at all. The person may profess to believe in God, but it turns out to be faith
in the servant of God. Or the person may be charmed by the
manner of speaking and be approving that rather than assent-
ing to the truth that is spoken. Some individuals are stirred
by the story of Christ, but in the same way that they would be
moved by a romantic fiction. In such cases there is no true

faith because the persons involved have no " relish " for
Christ's " sweetness," nor any true love for him, nor any sense
of sin. Rather, their pride is stirred — pride in their own supposed affections; and they do not deny and yield themselves
to God, but continue to deny him and his decrees.

The fullest discussion of the relation of faith to justification
is found in his famous sermon lectures on Rom. 4:5, subsequently published as a treatise. We may understand his conception by noticing the two views to which he takes exception, which views are far more common than his own:
namely, the usual so-called Calvinistic theory and the common Arminian view. With the former he has only a mild dis-
agreement, probably only with the language that it uses; with
the latter he has a far more fundamental difference which was
the occasion of his delivering these controversial lectures.

G. H. Foster (*Genetic History of New England Theology,*
p. 53) says that Edwards' explanation of the reason that faith
is the condition of justification " departs widely from the
mechanical methods of Calvinistic scholasticism . . ." This
may be an overstatement, but there can be little doubt that
Calvinistic theologians did not usually stress faith as a uniting
with Christ in the penetrating way in which Edwards did.
Nevertheless, he quarreled with his fellows mainly about their
mode of expression, not seeming to feel that they fundamentally misapprehended the truth of justification. Commonly,
Calvinists would say that faith was the " instrument " of justification, and the merit of Christ was the " ground " of it.
Edwards has this to say about calling faith an instrument.
" But yet it must be owned, that this is an obscure way of
speaking, and there must certainly be some impropriety in
calling faith an instrument, wherewith we receive or accept
justification; for the very person that thus explains the matter,
speaks of faith as being the reception or acceptance itself; and

if so, how can it be the instrument of reception or acceptance."

There seems to be no great difference here between Edwards and the Reformed tradition. The Reformed tradition taught union with Christ (although it did not always emphasize this as much as Edwards) and it also taught the imputation of his righteousness. Reformed theologians simply did not always connect the two so closely as Edwards did, as we shall see shortly. Edwards makes a refinement in expression, therefore, but hardly makes a significant departure. He himself did not seem to think so; nor has the Reformed tradition thought so. As a matter of fact, we need add only one expression to the Westminster Shorter Catechism definition of justification to make it fit Edwards' nicely: " Justification is an act of God's free grace wherein he pardoneth all our sins and accepteth us as righteous in his sight only for the righteousness of Christ " (WHICH WE HAVE BY VIRTUE OF OUR UNION WITH HIM) " imputed to us and received by faith alone."

We may note, in passing, Edwards' objection to speaking of faith as a condition of justification. " If it be that, *with which,* or *which being supposed,* a thing shall be, and *without which,* or *it being denied,* a thing shall not be, we in such a case call it a condition of that thing: But in this sense faith is not the only condition of salvation or justification, for there are many things that accompany and flow from faith, that are things with which justification shall be, and without which it will not be; and therefore are found to be put in Scripture in conditional propositions with justification and salvation, in multitudes of places; such are *love to God, and love to our brethren . . .*" (*Discourses on Various Important Subjects,* pp. 8–9.)

Edwards' great struggle was against the Arminian doctrine

of justification. He is speaking of the Arminians when he says: " Some that oppose this doctrine indeed say, that the Apostle sometimes means that it is by faith, *i.e.*, an hearty embracing the gospel in its first act, *only*, or *without any preceding holy life*, that persons are admitted into a justified state; but, say they, 'tis by a persevering obedience that they are continued in a justified state, and it is by this that they are finally justified . . . such a conditional pardon is no pardon or justification at all, any more than all mankind have, whether they embrace the gospel or no; for they all have a promise of final justification on conditions of future sincere obedience, as much as he that embraces the gospel " (*ibid.*, pp. 28–29). Coming back to this same matter nearer the end of his lectures he says: " This is the reverse of the scheme of our modern divines, who hold, that faith justifies only as an act or expression of obedience; whereas in truth, obedience has no concern in justification, any other wise than as an expression of faith " (*ibid.*, p. 84). And a few pages later: " The rewardableness of our virtue, is not antecedent to justification, but follows it, and is built entirely upon it . . ." (*Ibid.*, p. 88.)

We can see what Edwards is objecting to and criticizing so sharply. The Arminians, as he understood them, these " modern divines," were making faith into a work and then allowing justification by faith to mean justification by works. All the heart and mind of Edwards must have rebelled against this doctrine, for he believed that the best of men were sinful and could merit nothing at all, much less justification or a title to eternal life. And now the modern divines were making the crucial doctrine of evangelical Christianity only another way of preaching ancient Pharisaism and Pelagianism. It was no longer Christ who saved the sinner, but the sinner who saved himself.

But this still leaves us with the question, How did Edwards

himself view the relation between faith and justification? We understand what he did not accept as correct statement or correct doctrine. So we now should be better able to understand what his own doctrine was. " To be justified, is to be *approved* of God as a *proper subject* of pardon, and a right to eternal life: and therefore, when it is said that we are justified *BY* faith, what else can be understood by it, than that faith is that *BY* which we are rendered *approvable, fitly so,* and indeed, as the case stands, *proper subjects* of this benefit?" (*Ibid.,* p. 11.)

The difference between this view of justification and the prevailing Arminian one seemed to Edwards to be very great. " And there is a wide difference between its being looked on suitable that Christ's satisfaction and merits should be theirs that believe, because an interest in that satisfaction and merit is but a fit reward of faith, or a suitable testimony of God's respect to the amiableness and excellency of that grace, and its only being looked on suitable that Christ's satisfaction and merits should be theirs, because Christ and they are so united, that in the eyes of the Judge they may suitably be looked upon and taken as one." (*Ibid.,* p. 17.)

And then he continues showing the " twofold fitness " ("moral" and "natural") of justification. That is, Christ was naturally and morally fit for justification by virtue of his person and his obedience, while the believer became naturally and morally fit because of his union with Christ. He continues: " Indeed a moral suitableness or fitness to a state includes a natural: for 'tis never so that if there be a moral suitableness that a person should be in such a state, but that there is also a natural suitableness: but such a natural suitableness as I have described, by no means necessarily includes a moral." (*Ibid.,* p. 19.)

The Arminians were able to think of justification by works,

in their way of stating it, because of their doctrine of a new law. According to this theory, God had modified his demands so that fallen man could meet them; but at the same time he had provided the sacrifice of Christ to atone for their sins! This seemed to Edwards to be hopelessly inconsistent. " They hold, that the old law given to *Adam,* which requires perfect obedience is entirely repealed, and that instead of it we are put under a new law, which requires no more than imperfect, sincere obedience, in compliance with our poor, infirm, impotent circumstances since the fall, whereby we are unable to perform that perfect obedience that was required by the first law: for they strenuously maintain, that it would be unjust in God to require any thing of us that is beyond our *present* power and ability to perform; and yet they hold, that Christ died to satisfy for the imperfections of our obedience, that so our imperfect obedience might be accepted instead of a perfect . . . but if they are sins, and so the breach of some law, what law is it? they can't be a breach of their new law, for that requires no other than imperfect obedience, or obedience with imperfections . . ." (*Ibid.,* p. 27.)

Edwards, therefore, was dissatisfied with the Arminian view of justification on three counts. First, it taught justification by works, regarding faith as an incipient work and therefore the basis for justification. But on the other hand, second, while outraging the doctrine of justification by faith in this manner the Arminians then went on to make any true work unnecessary by saying that God had given a new law modified to meet our ability. So that works first supplant faith and then they themselves, on this new view of the law, become unnecessary. But, thirdly, in spite of that fact, Arminians still hold that Christ makes satisfaction when satisfaction should no longer be necessary since there is no sin to be satisfied.

Edwards uses an analogy to explain the way in which the

natural and moral righteousness of Christ are communicated
to the believer. " As when a man offers himself to a woman in
marriage; he don't give himself to her as a reward of her receiving him in marriage: Her receiving him is not considered
as a worthy deed in her, for which he rewards her, by giving
himself to her; but 'tis by her receiving him, that the *union is
made*, by which she hath him for her husband: 'Tis on her
part the unition it self." *(Ibid.,* p. 75.) The woman, by virtue
of her natural union with the husband as one flesh, becomes
also the possessor of all that belongs to the man: his position,
wealth, and the like. So with the believer: by his natural
union with Christ by the Spirit he becomes the possessor of
all the righteousness of Christ also. This is his justification by
faith or union with Christ. It is clear that it is immediate, perfect, and inalienable so long as the union holds (which, according to Edwards, would be forever).

But that raises the question, Suppose the union were dis-
solved, what would happen? If the natural union ceased,
would not the moral union also cease to exist? That is to say,
if the believer ceased to believe, would he not cease to be
justified? And if he ceased to be justified, how can it be said
that he is justified now? Would it not be better to say that he
will be justified if he continues as he now is?

Of all these questions Edwards was conscious, and to them
he applied himself. He answers all of them by calling attention to the nature of justifying faith. " God, in the act of justification, which is passed on a sinner's first believing, has
respect to perseverance, as being virtually contained in that
first act of faith; and 'tis looked upon and taken by him that
justifies, as being as it were a property in that faith that then
is: God has respect to the believer's continuance in faith, and
he is justified by that, as tho' it already were, because by divine establishment it shall follow; and it being by divine con-

stitution connected with that first faith, as much as if it were a property in it, it is then considered as such, and so justification is not suspended; but were it not for this, it would be needful that it should be suspended, till the sinner had actually persevered in faith." (*Ibid.*, pp. 77–78.) A few pages later he states the same position thus: " God, in that (first) justification has respect not only to the past act of faith, but to his own promise of future acts, and to the fitness of a qualification beheld as yet only in his own promise " (*ibid.*, p. 82). At the same time, we experience this forgiveness as the sins are committed, though the forgiveness is actually given in the first act of justification. This is the way Edwards explains the subsequent pardoning of justified persons after they have already been completely forgiven. It is subsequent in their experience, not in actual fact. And they claim the forgiveness according to the covenant of grace while fully ashamed of themselves for their sins. This point will be elaborated in Chapter XVII.

Another doctrine that Edwards teaches is the justification of Christ himself. Christ was not only delivered up for our justification, Rom. 4:25, but for his own also. He had to do two things for his own justification: one, fulfill the moral law, as the first Adam had failed to do, and therefore be rewarded with eternal life for himself and the elect whom he represented. Second, he, unlike the first Adam, had sins to atone for. While these were not his personally — sins that he was guilty of committing — they were his representatively. That is, they were the sins of the elect he voluntarily took upon himself. In that sense they were on him, and he had to satisfy their guilt before he could receive his own justification. " So Christ, our *second surety*, (in whose justification all who believe in him, and whose surety he is, are vertually justified,) was not justified 'till he had done the work the Father had appointed him, and kept the Father's commandments thro' all trials; and then in his resurrection he was *justified*. When he that had been put to death in the flesh was *quickened* by the Spirit, I Pet. 3. 18 then he that was manifest in the flesh was *justified* in the Spirit, I Tim. 3. 16." (*Ibid.*, p. 6.)

Nowhere that I have noticed does Edwards raise the question whether justification precedes faith inasmuch as Christ has already achieved it for the elect (as a number of Reformed theologians have maintained, such as A. A. Hodge, Abraham Kuyper and, latest of all, Karl Barth, the neo-Reformed theologian, who does so in a universalistic context). Justification seems always to be by faith for Edwards.

Since the faith that justifies is a true faith and is seen as such by God when he justifies the believer, Edwards stresses the importance of faith's being a working faith. " They that do truly come to Christ they at the same time take Christ's yoke upon them." (Matt. 11: 29.) In the application he urges his people not to trust in their supposed comings to Christ which may be nothing more than a " flush of affection." Rather, let them examine themselves to see whether they have counted the cost, whether they are laboring under the yoke of Christ. Any other type of faith is vain, he insists.

Noted as Edwards is as a champion of solifidianism, he bebelieved ultimately in justification by works. The only basis that justification could ever have was works or actual righteousness. Justification by faith is justification by faith in Christ's justification by works! " If we inquire what we must be saved for or on account of the answer is it must be for works, but not our works; not any works that we have done or can do but works that Christ has done for us." (Gen. 6:22.) The justification of the sinner is by his union with Christ, who is justified not by faith but by works. So in the ultimate sense of the word the sinner too is justified by works — not

his own, originally and actually, but none the less his own by
faith. " God acting the part of a judge determines and declares that men have a righteousness and so they are justified
by their works." (Matt. 7:21.) So the quarrel that Edwards
has with the Arminians is not that they teach justification by
works; he teaches the same. His quarrel with them is that they
teach justification by the works of sinful men, rather than by
Christ alone. It is not that they magnify works too much, but
that they do not understand that the so-called works of men
are in no sense adequate and that Christ's alone are sufficient.
Thus they give man a glory that he does not possess, while at
the same time derogating from the perfect glory of Jesus
Christ.

CHAPTER XVII

BUT NOT BY THE FAITH THAT IS ALONE

W E HAVE observed above that the faith that justifies, according to Edwards, is a faith that is seen by God as a
continuing fruitful faith. In other words, the believer's good
works are absolutely necessary to justification, although they
contribute nothing meritorious to it.

Edwards is always careful in his preaching to explain in
what sense works are necessary. One sermon has the doctrine:
" We should be willing to engage and go through with that
which is a great undertaking in order to our salvation " (Gen.
6:22) . There is a work that must be accomplished before we
receive salvation — ultimate salvation. Why is this work necessary? Edwards asks. He first affirms that it is not in order to
merit salvation. " Men can't [be] saved for any work of theirs,
and yet they ben't saved without works." The second reason
for these works is that " God for wise and holy ends has appointed that we should come to salvation in no other way "
but that of good works done by us. This God has done, not
that men may merit salvation, but that they may be prepared
to receive it as a gift. In the unpublished sermon on Gal. 5:6
we read that " there is no room left for any one to say that
they have faith which justifies and that they need take no care
about works and so to give themselves a liberty in sinning be-

cause they ben't under the law but under grace; for tho' 'tis only faith that justifies yet there is no faith that justifies but a working faith; so that it is as impossible that any person should be saved without works as if they were justified upon the account of their works. It is as impossible that men should be saved without an evangelical, universal and sincere obedience under the second covenant as it was that they should be saved without a perfect obedience under the first covenant." Obedience is as necessary now as it was under the old covenant of works, but not for the same reason (Matt. 7:21). In the old covenant life was to be obtained on the basis of works. This is not so in the new covenant. Nevertheless, in the new covenant works are required as the necessary evidence of the genuineness of the faith by which alone, men are justified.

The necessary good works must be " universal." " A true trust in Christ is never infused without other graces with it." (Micah 3:11.) This is the reason Edwards could preach that " a pretence of trusting in Christ is a vain pretence as long as men live wicked lives." Faith rules out such a life, for it infuses the virtues with itself. It aims at virtue as such and therefore at universal virtue. If there were any virtue that it did not love, it could not be said to aim at virtue as such but only some virtues, and these would be cultivated for some reason other than themselves; for, if they were cultivated for themselves alone, all virtue would be cultivated and not just some. " The graces are so related one to another that one includes and infers another." (John 1:16.)

Granted that it is necessary that a man be holy if he would see the Lord and possess eternal life; the question arises why it is necessary. That is because God says so, but the question still remains, Why does God say so? This question appealed to the searching mind of Edwards, and from his earliest preaching we have important sermons on the subject. For example, his 1733 sermon on Heb. 12:14 says: " None will ever be admitted to see Christ but only holy persons." A major part of the sermon is devoted to the " reasons " for this doctrine. But we shall consider more particularly another early sermon, on Isa. 35:8. Its doctrine is: " Those only that are holy are in the way to heaven." In this message holiness is defined as conformity of the heart and not merely outward conformity. Furthermore, it is a conformity to Christ and a conformity to God's holy law.

The reasons that Edwards here gives for the necessity of holiness are four in number. First, it is contrary to reason to make the wicked equally happy with the holy. Justice obliges God to punish sin, Ex. 34:3; Num. 14:18. Second, a holy God cannot embrace a filthy creature. It is impossible that God should dwell among devils. " It is therefore as impossible for an unholy thing to be admitted unto the happiness of heaven as it is for God not to be, or be turned to nothing." It is simply impossible for God to love sin or to love a wicked man. " It is as impossible that God should love sin as it is for him to cease to be, and it is as impossible for him to love a wicked man that has not his sin purified. And it is as impossible for him to enjoy the happiness of heaven except God love him for the happiness of heaven consists in the enjoyment of God's love." Edwards is here, no doubt, speaking of a love of complacency, not of benevolence. He makes the above statement more than once but he does not often take the time to explain the different uses of the word " love," though it is clear from his many utterances that he represented God as having a love of benevolence for the wicked and ungrateful. For example, the doctrine of the sermon on Luke 6:35 is: " God is kind to the unthankful and to the evil."

Thirdly, God could not only not love filthy creatures, but such a love would defile both him and heaven. It would fill heaven with the " loathesome stench of sin." And, finally, there is a reason inherent in the nature of sin which makes it necessary that the sinner be unhappy and incapable of being happy. That is, sin is a cruel tyrant, necessarily involving the soul defiled by it in misery. In its very nature it is rebellion and confusion; it could not consist with happiness. It is, therefore, impossible that an unholy person should be happy or inherit heaven. By the same token, holiness is necessary to glory.

In a later sermon on Ps. 119:3 Edwards gives six reasons for the necessity of holiness to happiness. We note the addition especially of a consideration of the Holy Spirit. This consideration was implicit in the former mention of the holiness of God, but here it is especially associated with that Person of the Godhead who promotes and infuses holiness. In this list Edwards also mentions the main principle of a Christian's life: namely, love to God which makes him utterly hostile to anything opposed to God.

These good works are not only necessary but they are very convincing demonstrations of the reality of Christian experience. For one thing, when Satan sees them he knows that he has been defeated and that one of his former captives is his no more. "When the professors of religion walk according to their profession God is so exalted by it that he thereby obtains a glorious triumph over the devil." (Job 2:3.) It is not profession that convinces Satan, but practical holiness alone. Such actual holiness is convincing to men as well as devils. "A manifestation of godliness in a man's life and walk is a better ground of others' charity concerning his godliness, than any account that he gives about it in words." (James 2:18.) It runs as a refrain through Edwards' preaching that actions speak louder than words. Indeed, the greatest test of religious experience (with respect to others and to oneself) in his most famous treatise on the subject, *Religious Affections,* is clearly this one (cf. *Works,* Vol. IV, pp. 332–416) .

One of the deepest discussions of the holiness of the be-

liever is found in the sermon on Ps. 119:3. The doctrine is:
" The spirit that godly men are of is a spirit to be perfectly
holy." Edwards observes that a Christian is never satisfied
with anything less than being perfectly holy. For him, remaining sin is a great burden and he will not be fully happy until
it is removed. He does not " allow " any sin, but on the contrary fights against all remaining sin relentlessly. He will not
neglect any known duty, for he is as opposed to sins of omission as of commission. He will make an effort, not to know as
little as possible of his duty, but as much as possible, and will
come as close to perfection as it is possible in his present state.
He loves the law and that not in spite of its strictness but because of it.

In the sermon on Ps. 139:23 Edwards compares the witness
of a godly life with the power of preaching: " If those that call
themselves Christians generally thus walked in all the paths
of virtue and holiness, it would tend more to the advancement of the kingdom of Christ in the world, the convincing
of sinners, and propagating religion among unbelievers than
all the sermons in the world, when the lives of those that are
called Christians are as they are."

As far as God, who searches the hearts, is concerned: " there
can be no acceptable glory and honor given to God without
grace. One truly sincerely person gives more glory to God
than a whole world of wicked men." (Luke 10:42.) Such a
person's giving a cup of cold water in the name of Christ
means far more to God than someone else giving his body to
be burned. Although this grace in the soul of saints is exceedingly small it is very powerful and, by divine constitution, indestructible. " Christianity consists very much in practice " and not merely in belief in doctrine and the catechism,
Edwards preached (Matt. 7:21) . It is a " very active thing
. . . always promotes? action." It is called a doctrine ac-

cording to godliness and it leads to a " laborious " life. " Faith
is a working thing." Although it is as a seed, that seed abides;
it is not destroyed. That grace is powerful is the theme of the
sermon on II Tim. 3:5. This is seen in the very nature of its
acting; truly Christians are baptized with fire. Its overcoming
all opposition (this plant cannot be uprooted) proves it further. And the fact that its working is able to mortify the lusts
of the human heart is especially evidential of its power. The
natural man cannot mortify his own lusts; all he does is to
close one vent and open another so that his lusts, if curtailed
in one direction, may continue to express themselves in another. Nor is reason and learning able to mortify lusts; not
even religion can do it if it is without grace. The preachers of
truth are futile against it. But grace can overcome this depravity. So we have a view of Christian grace that sees it, even in
great weakness, as greater than the lusts of the depraved human heart.

While the Christian has a new and powerful principle that
overcomes his lusts, these lusts are still present (Matt 5:27).
As noted above, there is not only remaining sin in the Christian heart, but there is more sin than grace there. The " natural distempers " (apparently he means those patterns of behavior to which some men are especially prone by nature)
also obscure the principle of grace, and grace does not always
shine clearly through them (Prov. 17:27). Furthermore, even
in the saint's most excellent experiences of grace, the evil
spirit is prone to inject himself. Edwards says that he has
known it in an abundance of instances that " the devil has
come in the midst of the most excellent frames " (II Chron.
15:1-2), just as Christ himself was led into the wilderness to
be tempted of the devil immediately after the coming of the
Holy Spirit upon him.

The inevitable result of the presence of these two diverse

and antagonistic principles in the heart is a bitter struggle. " That inward mutual opposition and strife that there is between grace and corruption in the hearts of the saints during their continuance in this world " is the theme of the sermon on Gal. 5:17, one of Edwards' fullest treatments of it. There is in the godly heart a struggle going on comparable to that which went on in the womb of Rebecca as Jacob sought to supplant Esau (Matt. 7:21). Warfare is another analogy by which Edwards was wont to describe the struggle in the heart of the converted person. " In order to our being preserved from destruction by our spiritual enemies we had need to behave ourselves in the business of religion as those that are engaged in the most dangerous war." (Eph. 6:11-13.)

The same truth is expressed from another viewpoint in the sermon on Luke 22:32. This sermon assumes that the believer will be defeated constantly by his adversary and must continue the battle and replenish his resources by a constant conversion by God. " Those that have true grace in their hearts may yet stand in great need of being converted." There are changes that the godly undergo which are spoken of in the like terms of the first change, which is commonly called conversion, Ps. 51:13; Isa. 6:10; Acts 3:19. The first work of conversion is called a putting off of the old man in Col. 3:9-10, but it is also applied to the saints in Col. 4:22 f. Spiritual resurrection signifies regeneration in Eph. 2:1, 5, but it also means later works in Eph. 1:6. Saints are exhorted to be transformed in Rom. 12:1. The Corinthian saints were urged to be reconciled to God, II Cor. 5:20. The disciples must be converted, according to Christ in Matt., ch. 18. On the basis of this Biblical data, Edwards draws two conclusions. First, any work carrying grace to a higher degree may be called conversion. Converts often call a later stage, their conversion, cf. Deut. 30:1-23. Second, when the godly are renewed after great falls this is called conversion, as in the text.

The reasons for using the word conversion in this manner are two. First, it is the same work of grace. Regeneration is sometimes called an act and sometimes a process, but it is the same in nature, Matt. 19:28. It is all a work of God, Phil. 1:6. Both the beginning and the process are called sanctification in the Bible. In I Cor. 1:2 sanctification refers to effectual calling, but in John 17:17 the word is used of an experience long afterward. Conversion is called creation, but every act of sanctification is a creation. And every act of sanctification is a raising from the dead. Long after the Damascus road Paul was still seeking to attain to the resurrection from the dead. Likewise the " putting off the old man " goes on all the time because no lust ever dies in this life. Also, there must be a constant crucifixion. Second, not only is the work the same in nature, but the manner of effecting it is the same. God again begins the work on the basis of an appeal to self-love and fear. Just as sinners are awakened in the first place, so they are subsequently awakened from their subsequent sins. Thus Hezekiah, after his great pride, was made afraid. David, after his adultery and murder, was brought to fear that God would take his Holy Spirit from him. Jonah, fleeing from God, is made to look again to the temple, fearing for his life.

But how does a person know whether his moral defeat is a mark of reprobation or of Christian imperfection? In the application of his sermon on Rev. 17:14 Edwards considers and answers this question. The saint may be deceived, he says, citing Noah, Lot, and Elijah as examples. A faithful man may be " surprised " and suddenly supplanted, or overtaken. But it is not the way of a true Christian to fall utterly away under ordinary temptation. If a person does that, he is not faithful — that is, not converted. This matter will be more fully discussed in the following chapter.

Edwards would have agreed with Calvin that justification is by faith alone but not by the faith that is alone. True faith works by love into obedience and good works. " All true saints justify the gospel of Jesus Christ," he says, distinguishing sound faith from Quaker " enthusiasm " (Luke 7:35). It would be utterly inconsistent for a faith that arises from a view of the glory of God and the awfulness of sin not to express itself in consonant works. What is religion, the Puritan sage asks, and answers it saying: it " is nothing else but the creature's exercise and manifestation of respect to the divine being " (Matt. 12:7). Let us not, he urges in another sermon, trust in any supposed coming to Christ. Careful examination will easily distinguish between a mere " flush of affection " and a counting the cost and following him (Matt. 11:29). True converts " take Christ's yoke upon them." It is a mark of true revival that there is a drastic alteration in behavior. " When the Spirit of God has been remarkably poured out on a people a thorough reformation of those things that before were amiss amongst them ought to be the effect of it." (Acts 19:19.) When the Spirit is thus come upon men there is a tendency to three things: awakening, converting, and confirming. " Some men are reformed, that are not converted but none are converted but what are reformed."

It may sometimes be difficult to know whether religious experience is the false affection of the ungodly, or the " dull frames " of the godly. Sometimes what makes a person want to go to heaven is really merely a desire not to go to hell. If in doubt, there are two sure tests: first, do you have some particular and lively exercises of the Spirit? And, second, do you prefer God in practice, Ps. 73:25? Edwards applies the Acts 19:19 text to his people: " It has lately been with us as it was in Ephesus. . . . Many things that were formerly found amiss amongst us have been in a great measure reformed and are for the present reformed. . . . It was much taken notice of amongst us the last spring and the winter before how much people's minds seemed to be taken off from the world." But, he continues, " 'Tis in the mouths of everyone how the town is growing worldly again, and what a great difference there is in the town from what was the last year." And he warns them that continued evidence of revival is necessary.

The godly do not only have a struggle going on within them after their conversion, but God sends chastisements from without as well. He tests grace (James 1:12). Edwards mentions various kinds of chastisements. We will consider here three of them: sickness, darkness, and affliction.

Sickness is given for purposes of chastening the Christian for his sinning, says Edwards, citing Ps. 107:7. In the same context he observes that healing is especially connected with pardon, Ps. 3:3; Matt. 9:2. So sickness may come from sin and healing from repentance. God sometimes resorts to this method of dealing with saints — inflicting sickness upon them — after they fail to respond to other calls, Job 33:14 f. The doctrine of the manuscript sermon on Luke 4:38 is: " When persons are restored from dangerous sickness their business should be to serve and minister to him that has restored them."

God sometimes hides himself from his people in displeasure with them because of their sins. " When persons depart from God after gracious manifestations that God has made of himself to them their sin is exceedingly aggravated and peculiarly offensive to God." (I Kings 11:9.) The light of faith will never go out, but saints may be guilty of shameful declension. As a result of this, God may deprive them of a sense of his presence. The saint will not then have that normal feeling which he has when in a " good frame." No godly person is always in a " holy frame " (S. of Sol. 5:1).

Third, and finally, God sends general afflictions on his sinning people. The early sermons on Ezek. 7:16 deal with this subject of God's judgments on his people, but also with what use is to be made of them. " God never punishes any man except it be for his own sin, and he suffers for no other guilt, but what is upon his own soul." Men may share in others' sins but no other way than by " making of them their own, either by promoting, assisting, or consenting " to them. This is true even with respect to the sin of Adam. " We are guilty of Adam's transgression not as it is the sin of Adam, but as it is our own as he stood our common head and representative and as our own souls by this means became contaminated with guilt and filthiness." So men partake of common judgments only as they partake of common sins. Therefore, it becomes all to mourn in time of general judgment. In the context of this passage some of Israel were visited while others escaped, and Edwards states this doctrine: " That at a time when a people are called to a general humiliation it becomes each one to mourn for his own iniquity." Thus all of God's people are to benefit from the divine judgments on any of them. It provokes God when his people lament public disaster and not their own guilt in it. The sermon ends in a call to repentance. The Holy Spirit has left us and general dullness prevails. There is an increase of vice and worldliness. Thus God is calling aloud for us to mourn our iniquities. Let us therefore in the midst of calamity recall our own sins. Let us " trace our own foot steps over again."

Although God chastises his people, he does not afflict them as he afflicts others. God would not let his people suffer as those whom he hates, says Edwards, citing I Peter 4:16-17. The same visitations are evidences of mercy to God's people and wrath to the ungodly. They work together for good to one group, for evil to the other.

Edwards preached often that relatively very few persons would be saved. Even among those in Christian countries and making a Christian profession few would be saved. " There are but few even of those that lie under the calls of the gospel that shall be saved." (Matt. 22:14.) In this sermon he observes, in passing, what he preached frequently, that none but those " under the calls of the gospel " ever are saved (he seems to have excepted some children, for he believed there were elect and saved children). But even of those who have the benefits of the means of grace and the opportunity of being redeemed, the vast majority perish. In his *Original Sin* he uses this fact as a proof of universal corruption. " Even these means have been ineffectual upon the far greater part of them with whom they have been used; of the *many that have been called, few have been chosen.*" (*Works*, Vol. VI, p. 214.) Many Bible passages are cited in support of this doctrine, such as Matt. 22:4; Luke 13:23-24; I Cor. 9:24. We find it typified in Isa. 10:22 and Jer. 2:3. The " remnant " conception in the Old Testament is appealed to, and the people of God are called a " little flock." They are the redeemed out of the world; the world itself perishes. Those who are called are like the sand of the sea to those who are saved, is Edwards' interpretation of Rom. 9:27 (Eph. 2:5-7). Most of those who hope for heaven are on the broad road to destruction (Matt. 7:13-14). Men are on this broad road because they are blind, and even the blind are able to find that road; indeed, they are born on it.

The effect of chastisements on the godly should be repentance and joy. Theirs is a true repentance, but nonetheless a repentance " unto life." How persons who have already been forgiven for their sins may yet confess them, repent of them, and ask for forgiveness is explained in a sermon on Ezek. 16:63. Saints should be continually repenting for their sins,

Edwards teaches in this sermon. Though these sins have been
blotted out of the book of God's remembrance forever, they
should not be blotted out of man's book of remembrance. Six
reasons are given for this doctrine. First, it is no reason for not
repenting that the punishment of sin has been removed, for
repentance is not so much with reference to the punishment
of sin as its nature. Second, the ground of repentance is not
removed, but increased, by the forgiveness of sins, Rom. 2:4.
Third, the saints are still sinful worms. Fourth, confession of
sinfulness especially becomes a humble Christian profession
and hope. Fifth, true grace tends to repentance, for it makes
men conscious of, and sorry for, sin. Sixth, repentance has
never been fully and sufficiently done.

It may seem strange that a man should rejoice in his sufferings, but that is the doctrine of an early sermon on Isa. 3:10.
" A good man is a happy man whatever his outward condition
is." Edwards first reminds his parishioners that the outward
circumstances of the godly are sometimes very afflictive. God
may send his judgments on the world without discriminating,
apparently, between his own and those who are not. So the
godly must enter the Kingdom through many tribulations.
But a good man is happy nonetheless. " A good man may look
down upon all the whole army of wordly afflictions under his
feet without concern." He is happy because he knows that he
is delivered from these afflictions and, more than that, that
they are actually working him good. What a consolation in
the midst of tribulations to recall that God is favorable to the
godly, even the one who " keeps him in being and who disposes of him and all other things every moment." This God
actually loves him. Affliction makes the saint think of these
things and thereby promotes his conscious well-being. Furthermore, these present trials accentuate the glory that is to
follow which will include the fullest measure of the present

joys without any mixture of grief. Such thinking, he concludes, with a very modern ring, is the cure of all earthly ills.
" Every Christian has the heart of a martyr." (Matt. 11:29.)
He need not suffer persecution but he must have the disposition to do so, if he is a godly person. In the sermon on Luke
12:4-5, Edwards shows that the worst evils that the power of
evil men can bring upon Christians, in the permissive providence of God, are absolutely nothing at all in comparison to
damnation. And since God is purifying his people by these
chastisements so that they may not suffer damnation, they
may look with calmness on the greatest of them. He goes into
great detail showing the terrible sufferings that the servants
of Christ have undergone; tormented without rest till they
fell; roasted until almost dead and then restored for further
roasting; tied to posts to watch their infants dying; frying on
gridirons; put in hot iron chains; their flesh torn off bones
with hot iron pincers; scourged till bowels fell out; cords
twisted about their heads till brains gushed out; faces chis-
eled; fingers pulled off with hot pincers; molten lead poured
down their throats; necks squeezed off between folding doors
— all of these things bore no comparison to damnation, and
the saints could properly regard them as but " light afflictions
but for a moment."

CHAPTER
XVIII

IF YOU HAVE IT, YOU CAN'T LOSE IT
(BUT HOW DO YOU KNOW YOU HAVE IT?)

FAITH produces good works — universal, continuing good works. The faith that saves is a persevering faith. " Persevering in holiness is absolutely necessary to salvation." (Heb. 10:38-39.) " 'Tis necessary for those that have religious affections and seem to have a love to Christ that they should endure to the end in order to their being saved." (Matt. 24:12-13.)

In *Justification by Faith*, Edwards gives the reason for these preachments (as we observed tentatively in Chapter XVI) : " God, in the act of justification, which is passed on a sinner's first believing, has respect to perseverance, as being virtually contained in that first act of faith; and it is looked upon, and taken by him that justifies, as being as it were a proportion in that faith that then is: God has respect to the believer's continuance in faith, and he is justified by that, as though it already were, because by divine establishment it shall follow; and it being by divine constitution connected with that first faith, as much as if it were a property in it, it is then considered as such, and so justification is not suspended; but were it not for this, it would be needful that it should be suspended, till the sinner had actually persevered in faith " (Rom. 4:5).

The same truth is stated in the sermon on Job 27:10. " Nor is actual perseverance necessary in order to a becoming interested in that righteousness [by which we are justified]. For as soon as ever a soul has believed on Christ or has put forth one act of faith in him it becomes interested in his righteousness. . . . But persevering in the way of duty is necessary to salvation as a necessary concomitant and evidence of a title to salvation." Furthermore, " perseverance is not only a necessary concomitant and evidence of a title to salvation, but also 'tis a necessary prerequisite to the actual possession of eternal life. 'Tis the only way to heaven, the narrow way that leads to life." If it is true, on the one hand, that " those only that are holy are in the way to heaven " (Isa. 35:8), it is also true that " perseverance in holiness is absolutely necessary to salvation " (Heb. 10:38-39; cf. also the development of Matt. 24:12-13). In a sermon on I Tim. 2:5 the certainty of perseverance is shown to follow from the union of the believer with Christ according to John 14:19, Rev. 1:18 and Col. 3:3.

Edwards often applies himself to the question concerning what may or what may not be consistent with a persevering life (cf. the sermons on Ps. 66:18 and Rev. 17:14). In the latter sermon he maintains that the godly may be deceived as Noah, Lot, and Elizabeth prove, but they cannot be led astray. In his " examination " he presents two criteria of judgment. First, true Christians may be " surprised " by sin, suddenly supplanted and overtaken in a fault. But, second, they cannot succumb to a practice of evil.

The argument for the necessity of perseverance is more fully developed in *Miscellaneous Remarks* (Dwight *Works,* Vol. VI, pp. 483 f.). Here Edwards presents ten considerations for this article of the Calvinistic system. First, God would not trust the preservation of the work begun by his own Son to man who, even in a perfect state, once fell. Second, saints are already " entitled to the reward of life " through the finished work of Christ. Third, without this truth there would be no assurance or hope; our joy would have to be in ourselves. Fourth, justification is by faith viewed as a persevering faith. Fifth, God allowed Adam to fall to show how necessary this plan of redemption is. Sixth, in John 8:31 only those who continue in his Word are Christ's disciples — by definition. According to I John 3:6, " Whosoever sinneth hath not seen him." Seventh, Prov. 24:19, Ps. 37:24, etc., as well as Ps. 51 (which shows that the Holy Spirit was not taken from David after his great sin), indicate God will not let his own go. Eighth, we need not pray that God would keep us if, as Arminians believe, we keep ourselves. Ninth, the Holy Spirit is said to be an earnest of glory. Tenth, Christ said, " If I should say, I know him not, I should be a liar like unto you." Christ, however, could not have lied. Therefore, such a text shows that hypothetical statements, which we often find in the Bible, are not inconsistent with contrary certainties.

It may be clear enough that, according to Edwards, if you have it you cannot lose it, but the great question still remains, How do you know that you have it? It has been observed that Calvinism shifts the point of anxiety from whether you will continue in a state of salvation (the Arminian problem) to whether you are in a state of salvation. This question greatly absorbed Edwards and much of his preaching is occupied with the crucial matter. We, therefore, now turn to the " signs " of regeneration. There are " distinguishing marks " of conversion. The book of Edwards by that title is well known. *The Religious Affections,* which is a fuller study of the marks of conversion, is perhaps Edwards' best-known work. In addition to many individual sermons on this theme, at least three important series were preached that are still unpublished: on Matt. 13:1 ff.; on Matt. 25:1 ff.; and on II Cor.

13:5. It is inconceivable that there could be the difference between the converted and unconverted that we have already noticed without some indications of the same to the persons concerned and/or to observers.

There is a preliminary question. Did Edwards regard these signs as the basis of assurance and/or an immediate intuition as the basis? Solomon Stoddard had originally preached that " there is no infallible sign of Grace but Grace. Grace is known only by intuition. All the external Effects of grace may flow from other causes." Though Edwards said things like this himself, even using the expression " there is no sign of grace but grace," he nevertheless criticized the writings of Stoddard because of this teaching. He noted with approval that his grandfather later changed his position, deferring to the signs of grace in addition to intuitions. This is surely Edwards' own position and it is contained in *The Religious Affections*. In a sermon on I Cor. 9:26, preached in 1741, he said, " Assurance is not to be obtained *so much* [italics ours] by self-examination as by action."

There are some bodily " marks " indicative of great spiritual workings. " A great fullness of the pure influences of the Spirit of God joined with discretion (?) will make a person appear and behave with that heavenly amiableness that his face will be beheld as it were like the face of an angel." (Acts 6:15.) In *Some Thoughts on the Revival*, Edwards defends the possibility of bodily effects wrought by religious experience. In *The Religious Affections*, he also defends their legitimacy but is especially anxious to show that they are not marks of conversion, necessarily. The position seems to be that bodily effects are possible, and in some cases even desirable, but not essential to religious experience, nor certain marks of it. He is opposed to those who interpreted them as proofs of the Spirit's working, and equally opposed to those who interpreted them as proof of the devil's working. In sermons such as Acts 16:29 and John 1:10 he spoke to this subject and, among other things, said that even extreme and harmful bodily effects were understandable though not advisable.

The spiritual signs of conversion are the only certain ones. They are easy to define but not so easy to detect. We hardly need enumerate these signs here as all the elements that constitute sanctification may be thought of as signs or marks of conversion. The great question concerns the possibility of discerning these signs and distinguishing them from counterfeit marks.

The difficulty is in detecting such signs. Edwards, having taught its possibility, urged the saints to get assurance. However, he raised so many problems that it became a byword that very few of his closest followers, if any, ever got it. The difficulties are formidable and numerous.

The first obstacle to assurance is that holiness is little developed in the best of saints in this world. It is " as a seed " (I John 3:9). Edwards often appeals to the Biblical simile of the " smoking flax," and in his *Religious Affections* he cites the famous work by Richard Sibbes with that title. For this reason very few are able to detect spirituality in themselves immediately (II Cor. 13:5). It is especially difficult to distinguish the beginning of grace (Matt. 7:15). A further complication is that " sudden conversions are very often false " (Matt. 13:5). It requires time, counting the cost and careful examination to find out whether the rain of God's Spirit has brought forth " mushrooms " or flowers (cf. the sermon on II Cor. 11:14-15).

Second, the grace that saints do have is always mixed with sin. The Holy Spirit is not given without measure to anyone but Christ, John 3:34. And furthermore, corruption tends to gain the ascendancy over grace in the true religious experience (II Chron. 15:1-2).

Theologizing more generally, Edwards said: " As in the first creation, God did not make a complete world at once, but there was a great deal of imperfection, darkness, and mixture of chaos and confusion, after God first said, ' Let there be light,' before the whole stood forth in perfect form. So in the deliverance of the chosen people from Egypt the false wonders were for a time mixed up with the true. When the sons of God came to present themselves before the Lord, Satan came also among them. When daylight first appears after a night of darkness, we must expect to have darkness mixed with light for a while before the perfect day and the sun in his strength. The fruits of the earth are green before they are ripe, and come to their perfection gradually; and so, Christ tells us, is the kingdom of God. The errors that have attended the work are the less to be wondered at because it is mainly young persons who have been the subjects of the work. And further, the situation has been so extraordinary that even ministers have not always known how to conduct themselves." (A. V. G. Allen, *Jonathan Edwards,* pp. 168–169.)

Third, assurance itself is intermitted. All those that are converted are not sure of it; and those that are sure of it don't know that they shall be always so . . . (Heb. 11:13-14). Edwards' general preaching tends to confirm his agreement with the Westminster Larger Catechism, question 81: " Assurance of grace and salvation not being of the essence of faith, true believers may wait long before they obtain it, and, after the enjoyment thereof, may have it weakened and intermitted, through manifold distempers, sins, temptation, and desertions; yet are they never left without such a presence and support of the Spirit of God as keeps them from sinking into utter despair." Viewing assurance as desirable, though not absolutely essential, to faith is another reason that persons would be far less certain of their salvation than if their salvation was thought necessarily to involve assurance.

Fourth, another difficulty in discerning the signs of conversion is the abundance of counterfeits. There are counterfeits of every aspect of Christian life. In his sermon on Matt. 7:15, Edwards mentions six points of likeness between the counterfeit experience and the real. First, the profession of hypocrites and saints may be the same; second, the things that precede and accompany grace, such as awakening, prayer, giving, etc., may be the same; third, every qualification of a saint may be counterfeited; fourth, spurious believers may be affected in a high degree; fifth, nominally converted persons may excel in outward things; and, sixth, they may hope along with the godly. Much of the ten sermons on the *Parable of the Virgins* is devoted to a similar study.

If counterfeits make it difficult for one to know his own spiritual state, they make it especially difficult to ascertain the state of others. Edwards makes the doctrine of his sermon on Ps. 55:12-14 that " men are not sufficient positively to determine the state of the souls of others that are of God's visible people." In this sermon he preached that the " corruption in the godly may go so far and is of the same nature with corruption in the wicked." He continues, " The more experience I have the more I am convinced." " All visible Christians," he concludes in the application, " have a right to be treated by the public as converts."

It is no wonder, he observes in another sermon, that good men are oftentimes greatly mistaken as to those that they look upon most likely to obtain heaven (Mark 10:17 f.; cf. especially Observations 10 and 28). Edwards himself is unable to escape the problem, for " there is a ministerial duty in dealing with persons' consciences and it ought to be left to ministers " (Ps. 55:12-14). Nevertheless, he has learned some things from his own experience. " I am less charitable and less uncharitable than once I was. I find more things in

wicked men that may counterfeit and make a fair show ot
piety; and more ways that the remaining corruption of the
godly may make them appear like carnal men than once I
knew of."

Five, the inexperienced and ill-informed status of the aver-
age person who is called upon to examine himself creates another hazard. If the job is difficult even for ministers and
revivalists as experienced and analytical as Edwards himself,
how much more so for the layman. Nevertheless, though the
church members should not judge others in this matter, they
are obliged, if they would have personal assurance, to judge
themselves.

The difficulty of gaining assurance does not preclude its
possibility. The real saint who doubts his conversion because
his fruit is so poor that he thinks he has none, is not to be discouraged. This, says Edwards, is possibly a proof of a " lowly
mind " (I John 5:2). And even though grace be meager, a
person can see enough to know whether he has it or not (Ps.
29:25). Assurance is attainable because the sign of it is no
particular degree of true grace (Matt. 7:15).

In spite of all the difficulties, assurance is an ideal to be
striven for. Five proofs are given of the attainability of assurance (Matt. 7:15). First, God grants all fullness needed to
the saints, and they need assurance. Second, provision for this
is a benefit of the covenant of grace, Heb. 6:18. Third, the
commands of Scripture, as in II Peter 11:10, imply it. Fourth,
reproofs are given for not possessing it, in II Cor. 13:5. Fifth,
assurance was actually obtained in various cases, as Job 19:24
and Paul in II Tim. 1:12. The sermon concludes with a number of rules to direct Edwards' parishioners how to obtain the
same assurance.

The " how " of assurance is dealt with in part of the series
on John 16:8 and elsewhere. In the John sermons this general

rule is given. Whatever convictions and awakenings are agreeable to truth and make men more careful to avoid sin and to use means are of the Spirit. Whatever says the same as the Word of God is the Spirit of God. Satan is a lying spirit. He that is not against us is with us, Mark 9:40. There is, in the sermon on Job 19:25, a long discussion of various directions for coming to assurance. But speaking generally, the formula is as cited above: " Assurance is not to be obtained so much by self-examination as by action " (I Cor. 9:26). Experience shows, says Edwards in one of his closest studies of this theme (II Cor. 13:5), that Christians who have passed from doubt into assurance exercise most grace. Life is most evident, in the summer when the trees are bearing fruit, not in the winter when the leaves are dead. In other words, the more grace a man practices, the more assurance he feels; the more assurance he feels, the more grace he practices.

Assurance is more than possible, it is relatively necessary. That is, it is a duty for a Christian to strive for it. " Persons ought not to rest ignorant and unresolved about their own state; whether they are real Christians or not." (II Cor. 13:5; Andover.) " Persons should be much concerned to know whether they don't live in some way of sin." (Ps. 139:23-24.) " 'Tis the most important duty of everyone to consider his own ways." (Hag. 1:5.) " Persons should not content themselves with that religion which they only hope will carry 'em to heaven but should get that which they may be sure will carry 'em to heaven." (I Cor. 9:26.) Persons must beware of neglect, as much as too much preoccupation.

CHAPTER
XIX

THE COVENANTAL FRAME OF REFERENCE

THE STEPS to salvation that we have considered are all taken in time. However, we must not get the impression that Jonathan Edwards thought of any of them as having been planned in time. Rather, they were the working out of the eternal purpose of an immutable deity. Therefore, if we would fully understand the evangelistic message of Edwards, we need to take a long look backward to the original plan of salvation in the eternal mind of God. And this flashback brings us to the eternal covenant of redemption and the covenantal framework in which man's salvation was projected.

The starting point in the evangelistic message of Jonathan Edwards is the eternal nature of God. If it had not been for his nature, God would never have created anything, including the world of men. Nor would he ever have created men except for his purpose of redeeming some of them. And his purpose to redeem mankind underlies the covenant of redemption which in turn is the framework within which the salvation of men is worked out.

So we may say that the salvation of men roots in the very nature of God. But what is this character of God that leads to the creation, fall, and redemption of men? This is stated most fully in Edwards' treatise *Concerning the End for Which God Created the World:* "To speak more strictly according to truth, we may suppose, *that a disposition in God, as an original property of his nature, to an emanation of his own infinite fulness, was what excited him to create the world; and so that the emanation itself was aimed at by him as a last end of the creation*" (*Works,* Vol. VI, p. 34). The thrust of the volume shows that God's manifestation of his own glory is not inconsistent with his seeking the creature's good, for the creature's good consists in sharing in the Deity's glory. "In the creature's knowing, esteeming, loving, rejoicing in, and praising God, the glory of God is both exhibited and acknowledged; his fulness is received and returned. Here is both an *emanation* and *remanation.* The refulgence shines upon and into the creature, and is reflected back to the luminary. The beams of glory come from God, and are something of God, and are refunded back again to their original. So that the whole is *of* God, and *in* God, and *to* God; and God is the beginning, middle, and end in this affair." (*Ibid.,* pp. 120–121.)

The first step in the working out of human salvation was the covenant of redemption between the Father and the Son. While Edwards speaks often of the covenant of redemption, especially in his *History of Redemption,* he does not mention the role of the Holy Spirit in it. It seems always to be represented as between the Father and Son only. However, in an unpublished sermon, the first in a series on John 16:8, Edwards deals especially with the work of the Holy Spirit in carrying out the covenant. "The work of the Holy Ghost as Christ's messenger is to convince men of sin of righteousness and of judgment." He "doth the finishing strokes" on Christ's salvation, and what he does he does as Christ's messenger. Ever since the fall of man, the Holy Spirit has worked subordinately to the Father and the Son. There is no inferiority, Edwards insists, for all the persons are of the same divine essence. There is no difference in glory. But this arrangement is agreeable to the order of the persons in the Trinity. It is meet that the one who suffered the great loss should have disposed of redemption. So Christ was given power over all flesh and the Holy Spirit was subordinated to him, whom the Father had made head of all things. Edwards does not say this; but we assume that he means that it was agreed by all three persons of the Godhead that just such a distribution of work in the redemptive plan should be, and each person acted according to the agreement or covenant made by all. Still, it is strange, if this is what Edwards had in mind, that he did not say so in his sermons on the subject.

This covenant of redemption is not to be confused with the covenant of grace (which is between God and believers), although the latter depends on the former. The differences between the two will become more apparent as we follow the discussion of the covenants.

Edwards speaks of " the Covenant of Redemption, or that eternal covenant that there was between the Father and the Son, wherein Christ undertook to stand as Mediator for fallen man, and was appointed thereto of the Father." Thus this covenant is not with man although it concerns man; it is strictly between the first two persons of the Godhead. In this same manuscript sermon on Heb. 13:8, Edwards refers to the covenant of grace: " Another covenant that Christ has regard to as a rule in the execution of his mediatorial office, is that Covenant of Grace which God hath established with men." This covenant is called an " everlasting covenant, Isaiah 55:3." It is the same covenant of grace in all ages of the world. The covenant " is not essentially different now from [what it was] under the Old Testament, and even before the flood; and it always will remain the same." Thus the covenant of redemption among the divine persons alone was, in the primary sense of the word, eternal; while the covenant of grace which was made by God with man is eternal or everlasting only in the secondary or derivative sense of that word.

In an unpublished sermon on Isa. 53:10, the *locus classicus* of the covenant of redemption, Edwards explained that Christ's seeing sinners converted and saved was part of the reward that God promised him for his sufferings. When did God make this promise? asked the preacher. His answer was: in the covenant of redemption from eternity. " God was determined that man should be redeemed and he in infinite wisdom pitched upon his own eternal Son to do the work." But this had to be negotiated by covenant, not by authority, for the two divine persons were equal in authority. The Son was appointed by command after the covenant had been made, only because that was part of the agreement (cf. manuscript sermon on Ps. 40:6-8). In the manuscript sermon on I Cor. 11:3 it is observed again that " God the Father acts as the head of the Trinity in all things appertaining to the affair of man's redemption." But it is to be remembered that this was because it was agreed that the Father should so act, not that the Father possessed any natural right so to do. If he had, a covenant would not have been necessary.

It is brought out in the sermon on Rom. 8:29 that it is the elect whom the Father gives to the Son in the covenant of redemption. " And this eternal foreknowledge implies three things: i. God the Father's choosing them and ii. His giving them to the Son to be his as he did in the covenant of redemption. Christ speaks of those that the Father had given him, John 6:37. iii. It implies the Son's accepting them and looking on them as his from eternity."

The covenant of grace is the means by which the covenant of redemption is actually carried out. In the latter, salvation is agreed upon; in the former the way of salvation is settled. The promises of the covenant of grace, or the new covenant, are expressed nowhere so fully as in Christ's farewell discourse, says Edwards in his sermon on John 14:27. There the Savior, after Judas has left and none are with him but those who believe in him, bequeaths to his disciples the benefits of the new covenant. These, here, include his whole estate: his Kingdom, his glory, his mansions, his life; peace, joy, grace, and victory. So the covenant of grace is that agreement which Christ makes with men: if they accept him, believe in him, he will give them eternal life.

Inasmuch as man is a participant in this covenant of grace, it is not eternal in the absolute sense, as we have observed. But now we must face another question. When was the covenant of grace agreed upon by God? Must that not have been, in the nature of the case, eternal? It seems clear Edwards meant that the Godhead agreed from all eternity that all persons who accepted the offer of the gospel of Christ would be saved when they did so accept. At the same time, it would seem that the covenant of grace cannot be thought to be in effect until the person believes in Christ. The elect are chosen from eternity, to be sure, but they are not admitted to the covenant of grace until the moment they accept Jesus Christ as their redeemer. When God gave Christ to die for the elect, he looked on them as they are in themselves; but in actually bestowing eternal life, he does not look on them as they are in themselves, but as they are in Christ. Explaining that statement in covenantal terms, Edwards would have said that the elect in the covenant of redemption are looked upon as they are in themselves — fallen — and as such given to Christ for redemption. But when these same elect enter into the benefits of the covenant of grace they enter into Christ and are viewed by the Father as in him, and receive the salvation that

he obtained as their covenant head. This is what Edwards
has in mind in the manuscript sermon on Gal. 3:16: " In the
divine transactions and dispensations relating to man's salvation Christ and believers are considered as it were as one
mystical person."

The covenant is compared to a testament. " The covenant
of grace is as it were Christ's last will and testament." (Heb.
9:15-16.) Christ's dying bequest for his people was that all
the benefits of the covenant of grace should be theirs. This
Edwards also explains in his sermon on John 14:27, discussed
above, where he calls the covenant Christ's " last will."

This raises the question whether the covenant of grace was
not in effect until the death of Jesus. Were the saints before
the incarnation and atonement devoid of the benefits of
grace? Were they awarded them posthumously? No, the benefits of the covenant of grace were in operation from the moment that man fell; but this was in anticipation of the death
of Christ. The benefits were administered in advance on the
supposition that Christ in the fullness of time would merit
them for his people. They were, however, awarded on no
other ground than the death of Christ. " For though the covenant of grace indeed was of force before the death of Christ,
yet it was of force no otherwise than by his death." (*Works,*
Vol. VIII, pp. 234–235.)

We have mentioned the covenant of grace as the implementation of the eternal covenant of redemption. There is
another covenant — how it is related to the covenant of redemption we cannot certainly say — which is historically
prior to the covenant of grace: namely, the covenant of works.
By the covenant of works the Puritans referred to an agreement between God and Adam that if Adam obeyed God for
a certain period of time, abstaining from eating certain forbidden fruit, he and his posterity would receive everlasting

life. If he disobeyed, he and his posterity should be punished with eternal death. We will compare this covenant of works with the covenant of grace, by which comparison its features will become apparent.

The covenant of works and the covenant of grace are sharply distinguished from each other, and at the same time they have some fundamental similarities. Commonly, among the Puritans, these two covenants are contrasted sharply. This Edwards also does. It is not so common to notice the profound resemblances between them, but these Edwards never ignores. We will consider first the differences between the two covenants, according to Edwards, and then the similarities.

The first difference we note is that the covenant of works was made between God and mere man, the covenant of grace between God and the God-man. The first Adam was a living soul, the Second Adam a life-giving spirit, I Cor. 15:45.

Second, the two covenants differed in the effects that they had upon those under them. All who were in the covenant of works perished with the violation of that covenant. All in the covenant of grace were redeemed by the fulfillment of that covenant (*passim*).

Third, the conditions of the two covenants were very greatly different from each other. One required works — the other, faith. Immediately following the doctrine of the sermon on Rom. 4:16 (" That the grace of God in the new covenant eminently appears in that, that it proposes justification only by faith ") are these explanatory words: " The goodness of God appeared in the first covenant which proposed justification by works. It was an act of God's goodness and condescension toward man to enter into any covenant at all with him, and that he would become engaged to give eternal life to him upon his perfect obedience. But the second covenant that God has entered into with us since we broke the first may by way of distinction be called the covenant of grace. The free and sovereign and rich grace of God appears in it in a manner very distinguishing. And the grace of God in it appears eminently in this that it proposes justification by faith alone." In the early manuscript sermon on Zech. 4:7, Edwards preached that if Adam had stood, he and his posterity would have been saved on account of what he did, in contrast to free grace.

Fourth, the subjects of the two covenants were not the same persons, exactly. That is to say, while every mere human being was an heir of the covenant of works and condemned thereby, only some of these were heirs of the covenant of grace. By no means all who were in the covenant of works were in the gracious covenant. As we have seen, Edwards taught repeatedly that only few, relatively speaking, would ever be saved, that is, be heirs of the covenant of grace. Another way of saying this is that all nonelect were in the covenant of works alone, while only the elect were in the covenant of grace as well.

Among the subjects of the two covenants, children have a different standing. All children, by virtue of being descendants of the first Adam, are in the covenant of works. Only elect children are in the covenant of grace. This raises the question whether children may be properly said to be in the covenant of grace without, or before, faith. Edwards believed that some were: namely, those who died before years of discretion were reached (Gen. 3:11) — but apparently he does not explain whether they were considered as special cases, or as having principial faith.

Children of godly parents were not necessarily in the covenant of grace. " God sometimes will withhold salvation from those, that are the children of very pious parents, and bestow it on others, that have been born and brought up in wicked

families. Thus we read of a good Abijah in the family of Jero-
boam, and of a godly Hezekiah, the son of wicked Ahaz,
and of a godly Josiah, the son of a wicked Amon; but on the
contrary of a wicked Amnon, and Absalom, the sons of holy
David, and that vile Manasseh, the son of good Hezekiah."
(Rom. 9:18.)

In spite of these numerous and drastic differences between
the covenant of grace and the covenant of works, they had
also important points of similarity. We mention here five of
these. First, each was between God and a representative of
human beings. Second, each had a works principle in it.
Third, each had a gracious element as well. Fourth, each had
an equivalent moral law as the standard by which the federal
representative was tested. Fifth, each covenant was revealed
in stages.

First, then, the two covenants had this in common: they
were between God and a representative, and not between
God and all individuals concerned. In this regard human
covenants differed from the covenant with the angels which
was individualistic. That is, angels were tried separately, not
corporately, and some stood while others fell. Each was treated
accordingly. In other respects the angelic covenant was not
unlike the covenant of works with man. That is, the outcome
was on the basis of works alone and the individual merit
gained thereby. The reason for human covenants being by
representatives rather than by individuals is the nature of the
human family. Men are affected both by heredity and en-
vironment and therefore are never, after the first pair, perfect
as they came from God.

The covenant of grace resembled the covenant of works in
a second matter. It also had a works principle in it. Actually,
each of the covenants was fundamentally a covenant of works;
that is, their basic validity rested on a works element. Neither

would have had any value unless there had been this foundation. Eternal life or death was offered, in the covenant of works on the basis of works. Adam and his posterity were to receive eternal life because of Adam's works or eternal death because of Adam's works. Likewise, in the covenant of grace, eternal life came to the Second Adam on the basis of what he did; although, and here is the only difference at this point, it is received by the elect on the basis of their faith alone. Still, the benefits of this covenant of grace came from works — the works of Christ. And these works are accredited to believers in Christ so that, indirectly, they are justified by works too. They receive their works (the works of Christ) by faith and thereby are justified.

The third similarity between the covenant of works and the covenant of grace that we shall mention is that each has a gracious element in it. If it is true that the covenant of grace has a works element in it, as we have seen, it is equally true that the covenant of works has grace in it. The covenant of grace is, of course, obviously gracious inasmuch as all its benefits come to the recipients, the believers, without their doing anything. It is all of grace. But it is also true, though not so obvious, that the covenant of works had grace in it. If we consider the disproportion between the eternal life promised in the covenant of works and the obedience required of Adam, it becomes apparent that such a reward for such a performance had a very great deal of grace in it. Adam surely could not have earned what he would have received for himself and those he represented, even though it was given to him and them on the basis of what he did. It is not purely of grace, as were the benefits of the covenant of grace; but there is much grace, even in the covenant of works (cf. sermons on Luke 17:9 and Zech. 4:7).

A fourth agreement between the covenant of grace and the

covenant of works, which Edwards observes, is that the law to which the Second Adam was subjected, though not identical, was the equivalent (and more than the equivalent) of that to which the first Adam was subjected. " There was wanting the precept about the forbidden fruit, and there was added the ceremonial law. The thing required was perfect obedience: it is no matter whether the *positive* precepts were the same, if they were equivalent." (*Discourses on Various Important Subjects*, p. 68.)

Fifth, each covenant was revealed in stages. Apparently Edwards thought there were but two stages of the revelation of the covenant of works; at least I have been able to find mention of only two. In the exposition of John 5:45, Edwards says, " The law which natural men trust in to justify 'em will only condemn 'em." This law is what the Pharisees and other Jews were trusting in, and it was nothing other than the covenant of works which was first revealed to Adam, and then more fully and explicitly to Moses. In his *History of Redemption*, Edwards remarks: " The covenant of works was here exhibited to be as a school-master to lead to Christ. . . . It was given in an awful manner, with a terrible voice, . . . the voice being accompanied with thunders and lightnings, the mountain burning with fire to the midst of heaven, and the earth itself shaking and trembling; to make all sensible how great that authority, power, and justice was that stood engaged to exact the fulfilment of this law, and to see it fully executed; . . . that men, being sensible of these things, might have a thorough trial of themselves, and might prove their own hearts, and know how impossible it is for them to have salvation by the works of the law, and might see the absolute necessity they stood in of a mediator " (*Works*, Vol. II, p. 76).

The covenant of grace was also revealed in historical stages. Indeed this is the basic theme of the extensive work on *The*

History of Redemption. " The work of redemption with respect to the grand design in general, as it respects the universal subject and end, is carried on . . . by many successive works and dispensations of God, all tending to one great end and effect, all united as the several parts of a scheme, and all together making up one great work. Like an house or temple that is building; first, the workmen are sent forth, then the materials are gathered, then the ground is fitted, then the superstructure is erected, one part after another, till at length the top-stone is laid, and all is finished. Now the work of redemption in that large sense, that has been explained, may be compared to such a building, that God is carrying on from the fall of man to the end of the world; and then that the time will come when the top-stone shall be brought forth, and all will appear complete and consummate." (*Ibid.*, pp. 17–18.)

In a manuscript sermon on Rom. 6:14, Edwards speaks of the " legal dispensation of the covenant of grace," showing that the covenant of grace existed in the Mosaic dispensation and that indeed, the Mosaic dispensation was a dispensation, a legal dispensation, of the covenant of grace. Like most Puritans, Edwards believed that the dispensation of the law was fundamentally a legal dispensation of the covenant of grace — that is, the covenant of grace administered in the context, or mode, of the legalistic system. As noted above, he also regarded the Mosaic dispensation as a second promulgation of the covenant of works; that is, to the self-righteous it declared the righteousness that would be required of all those who offered their own righteousness as the basis of their salvation. As such it was a ministry of death (though the Pharisees did not realize it) , even as the covenant of grace was a ministry of life.

We have indicated that the covenant of grace between God

and man was the implementation or working out of the salvation determined in the eternal covenant of redemption. Still, something more needs to be said about the bearing of election on covenant and covenant on election. Many students seem to assume that the two doctrines are incompatible. It is said by some that according to the doctrine of election God is sovereign and arbitrary while the covenant involves God in a contract and confines and limits him. One has God bound — the other, unbound. Many students of historical theology see the post-Calvin development of the covenant doctrine as a short-circuiting of the absolute predestinarianism of John Calvin. Some even represent Edwards as virtually eliminating the doctrine of the covenant (which we have already shown is clearly not the case), returning to the purer Calvinism of Calvin.

If God elected, he therein bound himself. He was arbitrary in electing, to be sure. That is, he did not need to elect at all. But as soon as he did elect to save some, he bound himself to save by some covenant or no covenant. He would have been bound by nothing but his own veracity; but he would have been bound by that. Having elected, he, if his word be true, must save. Men may not know what he has done. They may not know that he has bound himself to save them. But men's knowledge is not what binds God in any case. Only God can bind God. But this he does, in the very decree of election.

Furthermore, the covenant of grace is nothing other than the way by which God decrees to carry out what he has committed himself to do. He is already bound by his decree; this covenant can bind him no tighter. It binds him more specifically. That is, it binds him with respect to a particular plan, which he has imposed upon himself. The covenant in no sense " relieves " the doctrine of the decrees. The covenant, as Edwards and all Calvinists understood it, was for the elect and for the elect only. It may have been offered to all men indiscriminately; but it was wrought out with the elect in mind, it was applied only to the elect, and none but the elect will ever be saved within its framework. Edwards never labored this point, so far as I have noticed. If he did not, I think that there is a very simple explanation for that fact: he saw no reason to do so. It never seems to have occurred to him that anyone would suppose that there was any inconsistency between his predestinarianism and his covenant doctrine. For Edwards, the covenant of redemption was the covenant wherein it was agreed that the Son would become the mediator of the elect; and the covenant of grace was the way in which he would carry out his mediation for the elect. No reconciliation seemed necessary where no inconsistency existed.

While the covenant of grace was meant for and established with the elect only, it did bring some by-product benefits, called common grace, for the nonelect also. Edwards thinks of common grace as God's gift to natural men of temporal blessings, plus convictions of, and restraints upon, their sins.

In the unpublished sermon on Phil. 4:19, Edwards teaches that temporal blessings were promised in the covenant of grace according to I Tim. 4:8 and Matt. 6:37. The clothes men wear were purchased by Christ. Seedtime and harvest, and their continuance, are owing to Christ. Indeed, he claims in this sermon that all forms of the goodness of God to the heathen world were a result of the mediation of Jesus Christ. We may say that God's common grace for all men is an overflow of his special grace for some men. The covenant is the foundation, not only of saving grace, but of common grace as well.

Although God grants wicked men the benefits of this world, these do not actually benefit them. " 'Tis to the godly alone that God gives understanding wisdom to know how to use worldly good things they possess, and that he enables truly to enjoy the comfort of them." (Eccl. 2:26; Andover.) His second doctrine in this sermon is: " That God gives wicked men the travail and vexation of gathering and heaping worldly good things but 'tis not for their own but the godly's benefit." The wicked do not enjoy the temporal things that God gives them either in the future or even in the present. Everything they receive has brimstone scattered over it. They but eat and drink damnation as long as they remain impenitent. They cannot enjoy them even now because their conscience troubles them. If it does not, it is because it is hardened, in which case their pleasure is the pleasure of animals and stupid senseless beings. On the other hand, the godly do enjoy the very things that the wicked gather. They receive them with inward peace such as the wicked never have. They enjoy the love of God in these things which is infinitely greater than the things themselves. They have joy and thankfulness. They are wise to see the purpose of these things and realize them. And grace tends to prevent any anxiety or the like as accompaniments of these gifts. In an early sermon on Prov. 24:13, Edwards preached on religion sweetening temporal delights and observed that the wicked enjoy their pleasures " at war with themselves " while the godly eat their " meat with gladness of heart." Sinners enjoy with their bodies, but their minds suffer, while religion denies the righteous no pleasures but what have more of sorrow.

A more important form of common grace is the convictions of the Holy Spirit which God is wont to give to wicked men. " There are many in this world, who are wholly destitute of saving grace, who yet have common grace. They have no true holiness, but nevertheless, have something of that which is called *moral virtue;* and are the subjects of some degree of the common influences of the Spirit of God. . . .

Yea, those that are thus given up, yet have some degree of restraining grace, while they live in this world; without which, the earth could not bear them, and they would in no measure, be tolerable members of human society . . . but when men are cast into hell, God perfectly takes away his Spirit from them, as to all its merciful common influences, and entirely withdraws from them, all restraints of His Spirit and good providence." (*True Grace, Distinguished from the Experience of Devils*, New York, 1753, pp. 6–7.) " Damned men," he continues, " are not only absolutely destitute of all true holiness, but they have not so much as any common grace."

We may well ask why Edwards calls this common " grace " which issues in greater damnation. Because in giving these things, God grants the wicked a " reprieve from damnation " and an opportunity to be saved. That is an undeserved and very great favor which God shows them. It is a goodness in God that is offered to lead them to repentance, Rom. 2:4-5.

We have considered Edward's doctrine of the covenant that we may understand the frame of reference in which the various steps to salvation are to be comprehended. These steps are but the realizations of this covenant. While the covenant is not always, or even often, mentioned when Edwards is discussing these steps, it is always implicitly in the background of his thinking and preaching.

CONCLUSION

JONATHAN EDWARDS was an intellectual evangelist. Not only was he given to writing learned and profound treatises, but he preached solidly. He did not preach academically, certainly not pedantically. He made a distinction in method between the scholarly and the popular, but not in content. What he wrote in his treatises, he preached from his pulpit — and with basically the same arguments.

If it is true that an evangelist may be successful only in inverse proportion to the solidity of his message (which we trust is not the case), then Jonathan Edwards would never have been successful by modern standards, if indeed he could be considered an evangelist at all. He seemed to believe in the formula, " truth is unto Godliness," and preached accordingly. He preached the truth, the whole truth, as he saw it. And he showed the people why he saw it so. His sermons explore the nature of God, the essence of virtue, the fine points of salvation, the controversial issues of theology. None of these were withheld from his congregation, while in all of them he was urging his hearers to press into the Kingdom.

At the same time, as the reader will have observed if he has read nothing more of Edwards than the excerpts in this volume, the preaching was always clear. I doubt if any ever thought of Edwards as going over their heads. Probably, they often wished he had.

Edwards was a preacher of the Word. In all his manuscripts I do not remember one that does not begin with a text and its exposition in context. All of his " doctrines " are drawn directly from the text. All of his " reasons " are implications of this and other texts, except for a rare flight of speculation of which he was fully conscious and about which he usually apologized, explaining that he did it simply because some persons were more impressed by such reasonings than by the Word of God. He rested his final authority, however, on the authority of Scripture.

Furthermore, he preached every doctrine that he found in the Bible. His texts range over both Testaments and all the books of each. He preached about sovereignty and he preached about responsibility; he preached about hell and about heaven; he preached about grace and about law; he preached about individual piety and about social obligations; he preached about principles and about persons; he preached about terror and he preached about comfort.

I trust that this volume has shown that, in spite of Edwards' statements concerning seeking, he was a consistent preacher of Calvinism. He called no man master — not John Calvin or any other man. But, in the main, he clearly saw the Bible as Calvin saw it. This is not only clear from Edwards' preaching of sovereignty and reprobation, of total depravity and imputation, of efficacious grace and the perseverance of the saints. It is also clear from the way in which he preached human ability and responsibility. Men are unable to do any good thing, whether in the direction of salvation or in any other way. But they are able to hear the Word and they are able to do certain outward deeds that possess a nonmeritorious " negative righteousness." These things men could do, and

Edwards never let up in insisting that they do what they could. Neither did he ever cease to remind them that all they did was of no true value at all, could in no way recommend them to God, and did not in itself bring them one whit closer to the Kingdom than they were without it. In other words, he preached human ability and responsibility with as much insistence as any Arminian would do, but without a trace of Arminianism or the slightest compromise of his Calvinistic convictions.

Probably the most distinctive thing about Jonathan Edwards' evangelistic message is his theory of seeking. A natural man could do certain things (use the means of grace, obey the commandments outwardly, etc.) that would probably issue in his salvation. This theory falls between the Arminian, on the one hand, and the extreme Calvinistic, on the other. According to the Arminian theory of salvation, the sinner was able of himself alone to repent, believe, and be saved: all without the working of regeneration having previously taken place. According to Calvinism, regeneration must precede such gracious acts as believing and repenting. When the message comes to the unconverted he has no ability to receive it savingly unless God, at the time the message is given, works faith in the person. He will then evince this regeneration by believing the gospel which is presented. But if God does not work faith, there is nothing, according to some Calvinists, that the sinner can do. At this point perhaps the Calvinist Edwards is distinctive (though certainly not among Puritans). He insists that there is something that the sinner can do; in that, he agrees with the Arminians. Still, he denies with vigor that the sinner can do what the Arminian thinks he can do. But at the same time he disagrees with those Calvinists who say that there is nothing that the sinner can do. According to Edwards, he can do something nonsaving but promising and hopeful: namely, seek.

One last general observation about the evangelistic message of Jonathan Edwards: Being a Calvinist he, of course, preached election and the perseverance of saints. He also taught that assurance of salvation was possible and desirable. But here again he is somewhat unique among evangelists. The marks of grace and signs of salvation were so meticulous, exacting, and searching on the one hand; and the deceitfulness of sin, the counterfeits of Christian experience, and the difficulty of being truly objective about the state of one's soul were so great, on the other, that assurance became a relatively rare thing. Edwards himself did not have it before he was twenty-five years of age and never mentions it much even after that. It has been said that none of his followers claimed to have it, but rather remained dubious to the end of their lives. Here was a remarkable phenomenon: Edwards was a preacher who preached perseverance and preservation of the saints with unmixed purity, and assurance with the same confidence, while at the same time putting it almost out of reach of the most earnest. We can well understand the remark that was made about him when he was introduced to a congregation in Portsmouth, June 28, 1748: " They say that your wife is agoing to heaven, by a shorter road than yourself." The narrative adds simply, " Mr. Edwards bowed, and after reading the Psalm, went on with the Sermon " (Dwight *Works*, Vol. I, p. 285) .